Geoffrey Rootes' dream for

Linwood

TO COMMEMORATE THE OFFICIAL OPENING OF

THE LINWOOD FACTORY

ROOTES (SCOTLAND) LIMITED

ON THURSDAY 2ND MAY 1963 BY

HIS ROYAL HIGHNESS

THE DUKE OF EDINBURGH. K.G..K.T.

1

Geoffrey Rootes' dream for
Linwood

PICTORIAL LOOK AT A LANDMARK IN BRITISH CAR MANUFACTURE

Robert J Allan

BOOKMARQUE
PUBLISHING
Minster Lovell · Oxfordshire

To all members of The Imp Club — past, present and future
and to my Mother, who has put up with my interest for many years.

First published December 1991

© Robert J Allan 1991

British Library Cataloguing in Publication Data

Allan, Robert J., 1957–
  Geoffrey Rootes dream for Linwood
  I. Title
  338.47629222209411

ISBN 1870519124

Frontispiece: Linwood Commemorative Plaque [1]

LIMITED CASED EDITION

Page layout by John Rose
Edited by T. C. Colverson
Typeset by Bookmarque Publishing
Set in 10 on 12½ point Linotype Melior
Printed on Fineblade Smooth 115gsm
Published by Bookmarque Publishing · Minster Lovell & New Yatt · Oxfordshire
Printed by Litho Impressions · New Yatt · Oxfordshire
Bound by Butler & Tanner Ltd · Frome · Somerset

CONTENTS

ACKNOWLEDGEMENTS

IN PREPARING this book I am most grateful to the following people: firstly to Brian Postle and David Duncanson of the Sunbeam Tiger Owners' Club who first brought to the attention of the Imp Club the existence of the majority of the photographs used in this book. These photographs, and other literature now belonging to the Imp Club, are said to have been saved from disposal by Chrysler UK, when they were apparently rescued from a skip outside the company offices in Coventry. The photographs were clearly intended for press release use and many of them are marked and labelled as such on the reverse. Where explanatory notes were attached I have tried to incorporate these into the text, with some extension, to remain true to the original spirit. Secondly, my thanks go to John Rose of Bookmarque Publishing whose guiding hand has brought this book to publication; then to my friends in the Imp Club who have encouraged and helped me, especially to Bob Hawes, Gary Bond, Bev and Norman Stein, Adrian Thompson, Jacqui Clark and Peter Henshaw.

Photographs [10, 11, 37, 38] were kindly loaned by Peter Henshaw, and I thank the staff of the MIRA research centre for permission to use photographs of the ¼-scale model of the Imp.

Robert J Allan
Warrington, Cheshire · November 1991

Photographs and illustrations

Reference to photographs and illustrative material throughout this book is indicated by corresponding numbers [within square brackets] in the text. Numbers (within parentheses) refer to the specific sites shown on illustration number [28] of the Linwood Plant.

INTRODUCTION

THIS BOOK is a pictorial fantasy about the lives and times of the men and women who built the Hillman Imp motor car. It is mostly based on archival material now belonging to the Imp Club, and is reproduced with kind permission of Peugeot Talbot UK Limited.

In bringing this material to print it has been my aim to give the reader an insight into life at Linwood in the mid-nineteen-sixties, together with the social and economic climate surrounding it, and to let him/her come away with the knowledge of how a car factory operates, how it is constructed, how the cars are built, and even more—to understand something about the people who worked at this particular plant.

We will explore, by means of the photographs, the dream of an original team who were given a free rein to produce a unique small car. The team comprised of Peter Ware (team leader and technical director); Craig Millar (team leader responsible for the main concept and design engineer); Leo Kuzmicki (deputy chief engineer in charge of engine design); Bill West (transmission engineer); Ken Sharpe (chief stylist and development engineer); Harry Whyte (chassis engineer and chief designer); Mike Parkes (chief engineer); Tim Fry (coordinating engineer); together with Bob Saward (body styling); Bob Croft (body engineering) and C. Drury (project engineer, Pressed Steel Company). The initial design of the Imp had been made between 1955 and 1961 by Mike Parkes, Tim Fry and Leo Kuzmicki with the experimental facilities of Rootes's Ryton-on-Dunsmore factory at their disposal. The Hillman Imp was a radical departure from Rootes's tradition—its concept, design and history have been well documented in a fine book by David and Peter Henshaw, based upon their own research, *Apex: The Inside Story of the Hillman Imp*. The car's production was equally radical, as we shall see in the following pages.

Due to the efforts of Lord William and Sir Reginald Rootes and of Geoffrey Rootes (later Lord Rootes) a new model factory was purpose-built with government funding in a depressed area of Scotland. This was the dream of bringing employment and industrial success back to the Clyde Valley. It was the culmination of many years of government policy aimed at introducing large-scale car production into Scotland. Linwood then became the home of one of the most up-to-date production lines in the world for a car of very novel design: its engine, an all-alloy derivative of the featherweight marine Coventry Climax unit (similar to that used in racing cars such as the famous Coopers, and in fire pumps), rear-mounted in a monocoque shell and with all-independent coil-spring suspension and hatchback. The potential impact on local Scottish industry and the employment situation was enormous.

There is, however, no myth to the dream. Producing these cars involved hard work and tears: testing, retesting, redesigning, manufacturing and marketing to bring an engineering achievement into the hands of the unsuspecting public. Behind this lay the tangled political and economic web which ultimately was responsible for the misunderstanding and the demise of the project. Twenty-eight years later, even though the factory is gone, the dream is still there, with the performance, handling and economy also no myth, and the timelessness of a modern car which has now become a classic in its own right.

Danish journalists' visit to Linwood, 15 May 1964 (organised by the Society of Motor Manufacturers and Traders).
"A group of Danish journalists made a flying visit to the Linwood factory; they were met at the Renfrew airport by three demonstration Imps from the factory appropriately painted red, white and blue." *Left to right:* Jorgen Larsen, Bjarna Provst, Poul Jung-Jensen, Jorgen C. Pedersen and Bendix Bech-Thostrup (SMMT press representative). [2]

1

Geoffrey Rootes and the Dream

AROUND 1955 there had been a few ideas in the Rootes Company that a small cheap car should be part of their sales range. This was in line with the trend in other companies, and with popular demand to economise on petrol following the Suez crisis; the mass of sales was in the 1-litre range. Obvious contenders in the market were the Ford Anglia, the Triumph Herald, the Mini, and later Vauxhall when they followed suit with the introduction of the Viva saloon. In fact the idea went back as far as 1949, when the Rootes brothers William and Reginald were able to inspect, and were apparently very impressed by, a Volkswagen 'Beetle'. Craig Miller led a project to investigate the building of a small car, which was not subsequently continued. The line of thinking was later brought to a head when Michael Parkes from the design department was asked by Bernard Winter, engineering director, to carry out a new survey of existing small cars both in Britain and abroad, and a design study of how such a car could be produced, in which he was joined by Tim Fry. They were given free rein, and with startling results.

Acceptance of their initial ideas by Geoffrey Rootes and the Board of Directors allowed accelerated experiments at Ryton-on-Dunsmore as documented in the book *Apex: The Inside Story of the Hillman Imp* by David and Peter Henshaw. The Rootes product line traditionally comprised dozens of similar-looking, similar-performance medium-sized cars—Hillmans, Singers and Sunbeams, and also big Humbers, the favourite of Lord William Rootes. They did not have a car under 1400cc. Finally the situation was to change.

Geoffrey Rootes was to summarise this in 1982 "Rootes's decision to expand in the late nineteen-fifties was because of the growing importance of the small car market in the UK... and this was a sector of the market in which we were not represented. We had for many years been working on the design of a vehicle to fill this gap and the Hillman Imp was in an advanced state of design and prototype testing. It was for this reason that we wished to expand our manufacturing capacity which was necessary to fill this gap in our model range." [ref. 6]

At about the same time policy-makers in government were attacking the problem of regional disparity in employment caused by the post-war shift in industrial emphasis. Two active periods from 1945 to 47 and from 1958 to 63 led to changes in legislation to offer incentives for relocation and positive disincentives for growth in traditional areas of high employment like the Midlands.

Lord William and Sir Reginald Rootes, having decided on production of the 875cc Imp, based upon the prototype cars built in the Ryton-on-Dunsmore plant near Coventry, needed to find space for the project. Political pressure at the time, and the need for government help to finance the building work, meant that in July 1958 it was decided to find a site in Scotland. Linwood, 14 miles west of Glasgow, was chosen and negotiations with the Scottish Office of Industry started in January 1960. There were acres of ground south-east of the Ryton plant on which permission for development was refused. Instead pressure to go to a Development Area produced the decision to establish a new factory at Linwood. There was no cash to spare, so advantage was taken of a large government loan, which would have to be repaid at a large interest rate for at least a generation. Lord Rootes was a close friend of Harold MacMillan, then Tory Prime Minister, and entertained him several times at the Rootes's country home. He was able to secure the best terms for his company's development. Linwood was a suitable choice with a local labour force and nearby relevant industry in the form of the Ravenscraig Steel Mill, Invergordon Aluminium smelting works and the car body manufacturers Pressed Steel Limited who were already in Linwood. The final announcement to build was made on 30 September 1960.

The long-term policy to redeploy industry in Scotland had focussed attention on the motor industry after the reduction in armaments manufacture and ship-building. British car production was expanding in the late 'fifties following the Suez crisis and exports increased, principally to the USA. The presence of several major steel companies in the west of Scotland was an attractive feature of the offer. Merseyside was less attractive because of the competition from Standard-Triumph, Vauxhall and Ford.

The west of Scotland was the centre of the Scottish iron and steel industry. The Board of Trade persuaded the Pressed Steel Company to move to Linwood in 1947 after protracted negotiations. This was a crucial move for the government. The company, however, initially made heavier truck and railway wagon bodies in Scotland.

In 1957 the MacMillan government proposed to establish a strip-steel mill in Scotland, which would produce 3/16mm steel suitable for car bodies. Coleville agreed to expand their enterprise to Ravenscraig near Motherwell and construction of the new plant lasted from 1959 to 1961.

It was, however, more difficult than anticipated to get the motor industry to move to Scotland. Pressure from the Scottish lobby and the obvious political necessity to use the new strip steel mill resulted in the government giving almost a 'free ride' to any interested party, and very good terms for the local trade unions.

Geoffrey Rootes was appointed as the Managing Director of Rootes (Scotland) Limited to head the new project, and was thus made responsible for revitalising the Scottish motor industry and bringing the Hillman Imp to market. The son of William Rootes, he inherited the title of Lord Rootes and directorship of the company when his father died in December 1964, just after the launch of the Singer Chamois. Most of the photographs depicted in this collection are from 1961 through until 1964, and hence before the death of Lord William Rootes. It is, however, Geoffrey who features in them, and who was the guiding hand in the production of the Imp.

We see him first speaking about the Imp car concept with a group of visitors [3]. Next, we see him talking to Tam Dalyell, Labour MP for West Lothian during a visit of MPs to the plant on 3 July 1963 [4]. He explains the organisation of the factory, with the aid of a scale model in the main reception area, to the same group of MPs [5] and also proudly presents the neat engine compartment of a spotless showroom Mk 1 Imp [6] to, from left to right: M. J. Prior (Conservative MP Lowestoft), the Earl of Dalkeith (Conservative MP Edinburgh North), R. Gresham Cook CBE (Conservative MP Twickenham). The man second from the right standing next to Geoffrey Rootes is not identified.

3

It was indeed a brave, if somewhat misguided, decision to site Imp production in Linwood. It is this initial decision—with no clear social or regional planning in other related areas such as finance, transport, small industry or housing—not bad design or construction, which caused the ill fortune of the Imp.

Hood and Young in their book *Chrysler UK; a Corporation in Transition* said: "...it was clearly a mistake to locate a new factory with new labour force and building a new car at Linwood. There were too many imponderables and possibilities of error...". Likewise Peter Dunnett in *The Decline of the British Motor Industry: the effects of government policy 1945-79*, "...the whole Linwood project as a growth centre rested on the success of a single model. This was too narrow a base for regional expansion." and likewise, even in the *Rootes Group Review* (October 1964) there were some pertinent comments from Sidney Checkland: "...it could be argued that the entire Linwood scheme ought not to have been undertaken. But, given a set of circumstances that might have yielded success, it is difficult to see what other general course could have been followed. Conversely

4

5

6

it is easy to sympathise with the optimism which in the face of warnings pushed the scheme through, carrying the government with it, hoping that serendipity would produce unforeseen benefits." This was six years down the line and the stakes were too high to go back.

In the early days of production, therefore, publicity was the name of the game, both to encourage sales and also to further government and industry investment. Rootes wanted to demonstrate that the politicians had made the right decision, both for the car-buying public and for local employment, in order to justify the initial expenditure. The Linwood plant was a showpiece in more than one way as we shall see, and it is also clear that Geoffrey Rootes was more than happy to be informative and open about his work. It is perhaps due to this approach ultimately that we have a pictorial record today, and perhaps largely due to his pioneering spirit behind the Apex project that we have the now classic Hillman Imp motor car.

2

Making a Reality

BEFORE ENTERING the Linwood factory to look around, let us follow its construction so that we can understand the extent of the enterprise and its relation to local towns and industry. After reviewing the sequence of steps which go into mass-producing a car (see following chapter) we shall also appreciate how potential problems had been effectively solved in the practical layout of Linwood. This was a totally new, and in many ways model, factory which, however, keyed into its new environment—unlike the Ryton plant which had been built originally as a wartime shadow factory for Bristol Aero Engines.

We can survey the proposed site as it was on 6 April 1961, first looking west [7] from one side of the boundary to the fence on the left, the main A761 road from Paisley and Glasgow heading toward the horizon on the right-hand side, and the existing Pressed Steel factory on the northern side of the road. Looking east shows the site of the railway sidings in the foreground [8]. This railway would be the main connection to the Midlands, both for transporting the engines and for shipping out the finished cars. Looking south [9] from the roof of the Pressed Steel Limited building shows the entire site, still farmland but with the boundary fences and contractor's office in place. The almost straight road connecting Paisley and Linwood village appears to have a hyperbolic curve due to the panoramic effect of this shot.

The new construction by Melville, Dundas and Whitson Limited of Glasgow got under way in mid-1961 and covered 278 acres [10, 11]. A total of 450 acres, or

7

8

9

10

11

12

13

14

3 million square feet of industrial floor space, was occupied by the entire production complex. We see the factory near completion in the winter of 1962; again looking west to the transporter bridge crossing the road [12, 13] which brought the bodies over from Pressed Steel to the assembly plant, and south at the corner of the unit machine workshop [14], where components were finished.

As the opening of the plant neared, and actually passed on 2 May 1963, awareness of public interest grew. The commemorative plaque (see frontispiece in this book [1]) was aptly unveiled by the Duke of Edinburgh under the attentive gaze of the Press, and the Duke's drive back to Renfrew airport actually at the wheel of an Imp was sure to arouse interest. This was all well and good, but unfortunately it happened far too early and the cars were nowhere near ready to be launched. Peter Ware had pleaded for more time—up to six months to test a full batch of production cars, or even just a few weeks—and the engineers were also desperate to do more development work and testing. Ware estimated that this would be essential for the car's future.

Unfortunately the launch was already planned, and it was pointless to open the factory without releasing the car and starting deliveries, so the board of directors refused. This was ultimately the cause of bad press due to availability and reliability problems, and the car was doomed from the start. As an alternative to the required testing a group of apprentices was given the job of driving several cars on a round-the-clock basis, resulting in several amusing anecdotes related by the Henshaw brothers in their book.

Demands for information came in and the promotional material already sent out to dealers in the form of films, toys, booklets and board games was not sufficient—as shown in the letter now reproduced [15]. A series of aerial shots was therefore made around mid-May 1963 showing the now completed factory, and rather amusingly also the helicopter pilot and cameramen in their helicopter [16-18].

In this series the factory building has been completed and the Rootes name can be seen from the air in bold letters both front and rear [19]. The railway sidings at the rear of the plant are also finished and operative to take cars down to the Midlands. At the front of the factory—car parks, fences, the personnel block and grass lawns are also ready for use; only the underpasses on the main road remain unfinished [20]. Already some completed cars can be seen as we circle around the front of the factory [21], and also in the showroom at the front of the office block [22]. A wide view from above the Rootes Pressing plant [23] shows behind the factory the town of Johnstone, the railway, and the distant hills. To the western side of the factory some more completed Imps can be seen [24]—one is even being driven out of the door on the far right! Top left of this shot shows the die casting plant and the railway is at the extreme top of the frame. From behind the plant [25] the full panorama of the industrial complex is revealed in contrast with the outskirts of Paisley town in the upper right-hand corner. As we look straight through the central parking area we can spot a few more finished Imps [26]. The cars were in very short supply at this time—virtually all had been shipped to eager dealers to satisfy advance orders from astute customers. Finally we take a back seat as the helicopter flies out from Rootes Limited [27], turns full circle and retreats once more over the town of Paisley. The last shot was actually made at a different time from the preceding ones and does not follow the same sequence. We see that the underpass in the main road has been finished, and this road now became a fast dual carriageway with facilities for traffic between the two plants.

15

ROOTES GROUP

Internal Memo

To   Mrs. J. Wilkinson
Devonshire House

From   Mr. G.W. Ashby
Group Advertising
Devonshire House

Date   16 May, 1963.

GWA/1603

c.c. Mr. W. Elsey
Mr. L. Hunter
Mr. L.A. Wise

AERIAL PHOTOGRAPHS - LINWOOD

     I don't know if you may have noticed in our promotion material on the Imp but we have offered dealers both cinema and television filmlets which include aerial views of the new factory.

     When these were shot from the helicopter, we asked for stills to be taken. I am now enclosing these, in colour and in black and white, in case you may possibly be able to make use of them.

     Would you please let me have two copies each of 8.6 and B.7.

16   17   18

19

20

21

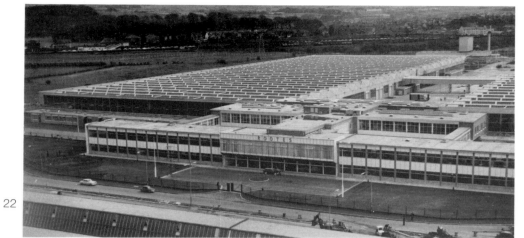

22

23

24

25

26

27

28

3

Working at Rootes, Linwood

WE NOW turn our attention to activity inside the factory.
A close study of the photographs reveals details of the assembly sequence by which the cars were built up. Perhaps most interesting is the steel shell itself, which was built in the adjacent factory of Pressed Steel Limited (number 8 on the line drawing [28]) and conveyed to the car assembly block (6) where the final components were fitted by overhead transporter.

Engine and component production was a different matter, and some pictures of it appear in the Henshaws' book. A novel feature of the Imp was the manufacture using die-cast aluminium alloy components, and the provision of a special plant and equipment at Linwood to carry this out (3). This cost £1·25 million and was unique to British car plants. It was separate from the main factory, for reasons of safety, but on the main site, whereas the pressings factory was on the opposite side of the main road and connected by transporter bridge and subways. Complete cylinder blocks were die cast, as were all other components except for the cylinder head.

The main plant was destined to be entirely self-contained [29], and indeed the whole factory operated as self-sufficiently as possible, except for the bought-in components described in a later chapter. A photograph shows the central service tunnel which housed air, gas, electricity and water supplies for easy accessibility.

Let us drive inside the factory and have a look around. We approach the plant by car from Linwood [30], and are obliged to pass Rootes Pressings Limited (the Pressed Steel Company prior to 1966) [31] before taking the underpass into the main gate. We will first stop outside the building which houses the die-casting division [32], managed by Jim Shaw.

The first photograph I have chosen to illustrate the inside of this building dates from 12 January 1965 [33]; and the original text is quoted: "During his tour of Scottish industries Mr William Ross, Secretary of State for Scotland, to-day visited the Rootes Group's factory at Linwood, near Paisley.

"He was greeted by Lord Rootes, Chairman of Rootes (Scotland) Limited and Mr G. H. B. Cattell, Director and Manager of the Company.

"Mr Ross was accompanied by Mr J. Bennett, his Parliamentary Private Secretary; Mr N. Baird, his Private Secretary; Miss Betty Harvie Anderson, MP for East Renfrewshire and Mr Norman Buchan, MP for West Renfrewshire. They inspected the die-casting plant, the machine shop and the final assembly track.

29

30

31

32

"The party also included Mr C. Whitehouse (Board of Trade), Mr McGuiness of the Scottish Development Department, Mr W. Ballantyre of the Scottish Information Office, Mr P. L. Griffiths, Director and General Manager of Pressed Steel Company, Linwood, and Mr R. Davies, Assistant Managing Director of Pressed Steel Company Limited, Cowley."

The men are pictured standing next to, not a pile of bullion, but aluminium bars, made by British Aluminium Company, Invergordon, ready to be smelted down to start the casting process. This tour of important visitors is typical of many tours around Linwood in the early days, as will be illustrated in the following chapters.

The next few photographs highlight the technical nature of the business. First comes the line of bulk melting furnaces [34], handling 3½ tons of aluminium per hour. The metal storage area is immediately behind, and consumption was approximately one hundred tons per week. We next walk down the main aisle in the die-casting plant [35]. A man is seen with a stacker truck carrying a crucible of molten aluminium to be poured into the pressurised casting machine. One hundred to six hundred ton pressure die-casting machines from the Swiss Buhler company were used. Each machine carried a different number, had an operator, and produced a different component for the Imp. The functional layout of the plant was impressive, its clean, light and uncluttered atmosphere was partly due to the use of aluminium rather than iron, the former having a lower melting point.

Another advantage of aluminium in car production is the resulting very light weight of the power unit and transaxle which endowes the Imp with its extremely good handling capability. Heat dissipation from aluminium components is also good, but engine noises may be more audible. To the car's owner the bright shiny appearance of the aluminium engine must be of interest; on the other hand the use of this somewhat novel material (for the nineteen-sixties) required the owner to maintain his new car carefully, regularly checking oil level and ethylene-glycol content of the coolant so that the aluminium would not corrode on contact with water and ultimately overheat and distort. This was never a problem with the prototype cars which covered thousands of miles of fast motoring. Not all owners proved, however, to be as responsible in maintenance as the company would have liked, nor was production as good, and the new engines soon obtained a bad, but unwarranted, reputation.

Shown [36] is a selection of aluminium alloy castings made at the Linwood die-casting division for the Hillman Imp and its derivatives. Left to right: first row: hypoid casting, clutch housing, cylinder block. Second row: gearbox mounting cover, cambox cover, timing cover. Third row: gearbox casing, front mounting bracket, tappet block, clamp rack and pinion (slightly lower in picture), engine mounting rear. Fourth row: induction manifold, front bearing cap, centre bearing cap, rear bearing cap. Fifth row: oil filler pipe, water inlet pipe, water pump body inlet, water pump body outlet. These are all Mk 1 components, as indeed are most of the cars shown in this book; some were later modified as demand or economics required. Die-castings were also made for other companies, such as Hoover Limited, Cambuslang.

The original Coventry Climax engine was sand cast and therefore, although it was made of aluminium alloy, it had a relatively heavy cylinder block. This had to be converted to a lighter die-cast unit for volume production and improved handling in the rear location, and Peter Ware and Bill Bryant (Managing Director of Hills Precision who made some components for the prototype bodyshell) assessed the best process for this in 1961. It was the first time that a British volume car manufacturer had used an all-alloy engine, and Rootes's engineers at first had little knowledge of the processes of working with this material. The Climax engine was redesigned by Leo Kuzmicki and the original cylinder blocks for the prototypes were machined from steel by Coventry Climax. Later ones were low-pressure die-cast by the Northamptonshire firm of Alumasc. Leo Kuzmicki had worked for other engine manufacturers and faced this job with no difficulty. His association with the Climax engine was also a long one. One of his contributions to British motor sport was to design the four-cylinder 2-litre Vandervell engine based on the Norton alloy cylinder head and piston design. This engine was put into a Cooper body (John Cooper also used an engine adapted from the Coventry Climax unit, but in 2-litre form) and became the Vanwall Special, the inspiration of Thomas Vandervell.

33

34

35

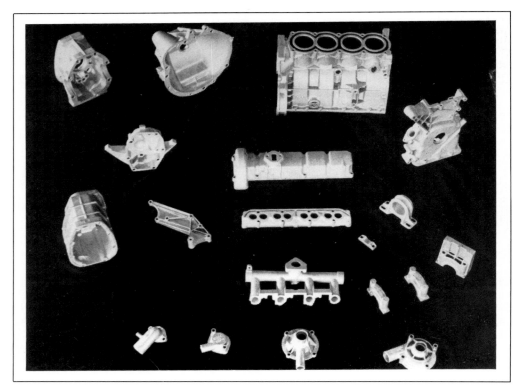

36

Actual die-casting of the cylinder blocks in the Linwood plant is shown in the photographs from Peter Henshaw's collection: firstly inserting the iron cylinder liners into the mould [37] and then removing the finished block [38]. In production die-cast components were carefully scrutinised to avoid costly faults coming to light at a later stage. Shown is an employee of the die-casting division checking the dimensional accuracy of an engine block before machining has taken place [39]. Other samples were subjected to X-ray examination [40]. Porosity bubbles hidden inside the castings were the main worry. These show up in the X-ray as light or shaded areas.

Once a run of castings was in hand, inspection of every tenth casting would be enough, with back-tracking if a fault should show. Some castings such as the main bearing caps were one hundred per cent inspected, since bearings 'letting go' during use could be catastrophic. Batches of the material itself, the melts of aluminium alloy from the furnaces, were each analysed, a sample being electrically sparked (burned) to produce a vapour in which the spectrum of each of its eleven or so constituent elements may be recognised by its characteristic colour, just as the green colour of copper can be seen in a flame, for instance. The intensity of each part of the spectrum is proportional to the amount of the corresponding element present in the mix, and this was analysed by a triple-medium direct-reading spectrograph with automatic digital output, from Hilger and Watts. Confirmation of the correct alloy, or adjustments to it, were thus available within minutes—allowing a very tight control.

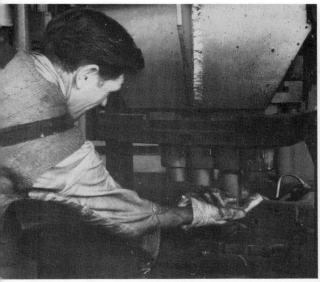

37

38

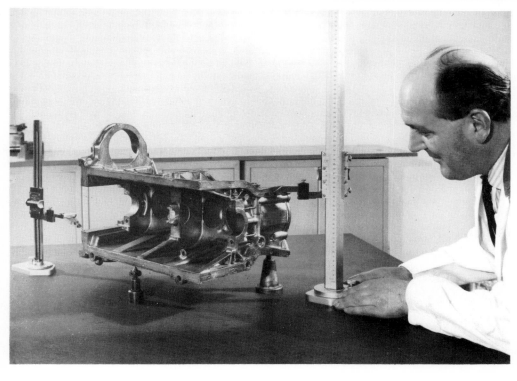

39

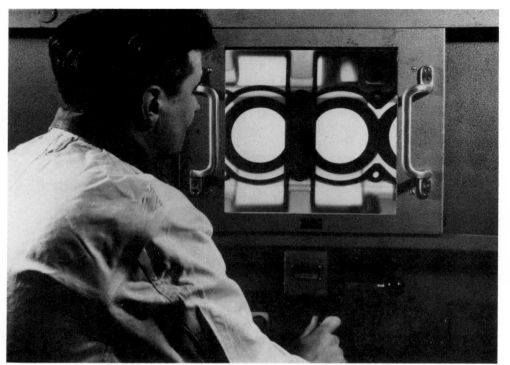

40

41

The cylinder head was not made at Linwood, but was sand-cast by Aeroplane and Motor Aluminium Castings in Birmingham; A & M also made alloy heads for the Sunbeam Rapier and Alpine engines, using gravity feed casting principles. This expensive and time-consuming process was also used for the original Coventry Climax FWMA engine from which the Imp unit was derived. Because of the complex construction of the head the process had to be continued, and for this reason, and because of expertise in building engines at the Ryton plant near Coventry, the blocks and components were shipped down for assembly and testing, and then later sent back in crates to Linwood to be installed into the cars. The crankshaft was also made near to Coventry. Every Imp engine has travelled some 300 miles further than the car into which it was originally installed!

Moving now into the unit machine shop (4) we first see the control room where things were kept running smoothly [41]. Die-castings were brought in from the adjacent building along with other raw materials, and built-up engines returned from Ryton. These would be fitted to the complete rear assembly and transaxle which were all produced in Linwood.

Fantastic machines were used for these workshop operations. One was the Archdale Transfer Machine where rear suspension arms were automatically passed through each of eleven machining operations [42]. Another was the Churchill Link Line, on which nine machines linked by automatic conveyors carried out consecutive operations to produce completed final drive units for the gearbox. Lord Rootes and the party with Mr William Ross (mentioned earlier) are shown inspecting the results of this process [43, 44, 45]. Some components needed to be heat-treated in order to harden them. In the Metal Hardening Plant area this heat treatment embodied the very latest process [46, 47]. A final machine illustrated is the Ryder automatic rotary machine [48]. On this, brake drums for the Hillman Imp were machined.

The finished units were transferred to the main assembly area (6) by a special conveyor bridge and there met the steel bodyshells. The latter started life across the road at Pressed Steel Limited as metal panels cut from vast coils of sheet steel. The coils, weighing about 10 tons each, arrived from Colville's Ravenscraig hot strip mills just 30 miles away. Around 6,000 men were employed by Pressed Steel, of whom one third worked on the Imp body production: as many as in the assembly plant itself.

The Imp bodyshell was a pretty good one for 1963, though at first it suffered from water leaks, but by production standards of the late nineteen-sixties it was already complicated and heavy. The owner did not have to worry about the Rootes cars since he/she was getting strength and rigidity overspecified at the manufacturers' cost. Even the lighter panels and less painstaking construction technique used by Chrysler after 1967 left the shell strong enough for most normal purposes, bearing out the correctness of the original design. It is, however, imperative that the original criteria be adhered to when panels are replaced on cars requiring restoration. This is particularly true in the sill area which endows the Imp with its natural strength and rigidity and therefore its characteristically good handling.

Several changes were made between 1963 and 1965 to eliminate leaks and to

42

43

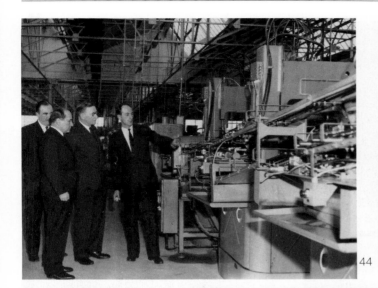

44

45

46

47

48

protect the body. With the introduction of the more expensive Chamois and Super Imp Mk 2 in October 1964 just before the death of Lord William Rootes, a lot of additional sound proofing was also provided. A new quality control department, managed by Jim Lauder, operated since the summer of 1964 and this aimed to eliminate, by a combination of measures, all the original troubles which had been brought to light over the past year. There were a series of random and regular dimension checks on windscreen and window apertures at the sub-assembly stage, and on the build-up and final assembly lines. This was the first step in ensuring that joints would be waterproof. Visual inspections for condition were also made at each stage.

Sealing and underbody protection became increasingly important with the growing use of salt during winter months on British roads in the nineteen-sixties. The early Imp family was one of the best protected, if not the best protected, of all small cars, and this has resulted in the longevity of many pre-1967 examples. Inadequate sealing was never a problem except on very early Mk 1 cars.

Sealing compound was applied first, at the sub-assembly stage, between vulnerable panel joints such as those around the wheel arches and the posts supporting the doors. These had to be treated in the early stages while they were still accessible. Hidden surfaces and pockets in the body were given a coat of zinc-based primer before the parts were welded together.

Later when the bodyshell had been welded up black 'Expandite' compound was applied on the inside to all the joints around the floor, wheel arches and the rear seat pan. The rubber seals holding the screen and rear window glasses were also given sealer underneath the adhesive on the Mk 1 cars.

The procedure for building the shell was firstly to put together floorpan, chassis rails, sills (inner and outer), wheel arches, bulkheads, door pillars and frames and rear frame. Next the front window frame and the wings were fitted. At this stage the entire bodyshell and the transporting railway carriage to which it was attached could be inverted in a special cage for underframe welding [49]. After this the transom and doors were fitted temporarily so that the shell could be painted.

In the paint shop the bodyshells underwent several independent protective treatments after they had been washed and degreased. The order of treatment was to apply phosphate, slipper-dip prime, heavy sealing compound to the whole underneath, sand wet, apply sealing compound to interior joints, paint and bake, sand wet, apply sealing compound to interior joints, paint and bake, sand dry, apply two coats of colour (wet on wet), bake.

An example of the care needed in the process and the complexity of the causes of paint imperfections is an early trouble of interlayer pollution. Detective work eventually showed this to be the result of invisible atmospheric pollution arising from silicon-grease-based products used in earlier sections of the factory. This highlights the amazing number of factors which need to be accounted for, and may sometimes be overlooked, in designing a car factory!

Most of the paint processes were standard practice in the mid-nineteen-sixties. Some manufacturers even subjected their cars to a full rotary dip rather than the slipper dip which gave protection only below the waist line (where, of course, it

49

is most needed). The extent of underside treatment, involving the spraying on of 33lbs of bituminous material was, however, rather exceptional, and was intended partly as an insurance against the earlier leak problems as well as to combat corrosion. It also made the cars quieter to drive by preventing drumming of the floor pan, as did the similar amount of bitumen inside the car. Leak problems have recurred in most Imps surviving to this day as the original material has fallen off or captured moisture and spot-welded joints have opened up.

The next job was to install windows, door mechanism and handles, wiring harness, hoses and exterior trim. This was also carried out on small specially-designed railway carriages which were transported around the factory. Moving

50

the shells onto an overhead conveyor allowed work to be done on the underside. This included drilling holes for the suspension, fitting brake pipes, cables and fuel pipe. The body leaving Pressed Steel was almost a saleable kit car, requiring just installation of the suspension, engine and gearbox. This was the same procedure as for production of the Hillman Minx and Singer Gazelle at Cowley, and it was partly because Rootes had so little capital available that they could not do the full job themselves.

As each bodyshell left Pressed Steel to cross the road by conveyor bridge, it triggered a data-processing system to coordinate the flow of components on the main assembly line. An electronic system then controlled the central conveyor [50]. Controls in the main assembly building were supplied by MTE Control Gear Limited, to the order of Geo. W. King Limited. Feed-in rate of bodyshells was indicated on the control console. Each conveyor could be controlled individually or in logical groups from the latter. Motor control gear was housed in the surrounding panels.

Shells were kept on the overhead transporter slings [51] to equalise movements in the two plants. After this, bodies were dropped onto the already prepared suspension and transmission components and the empty slings were returned to the pressings plant. Front and rear mechanical assemblies upon which the body was mounted were treated to 'Astrolan' protective finish. The shells were dropped onto the complete front suspension and complete rear suspension transmission and engine assembly which were built up in a separate area. After the 'dropping' the final assembly could take place on the main track [52]. Operators at their 'work stations' completed the cars by taking components from specially designed containers which were easily accessible. This final low-level 'main assembly' conveyor allowed work to be completed in fitting lights, interior, fuel tanks and other accessories. The wheels were put on last so that the cars could be driven out and tested.

At the end of the line qualified mechanics drove the cars off onto rear wheel rollers. Here they received their first running checks and any obvious fault was found and diagnosed. The engines had been turning before this and one in ten had been run and been power-tested. Part of this testing of the car included a high pressure water jet blast to check for leaks in the bodywork. A single spray was not enough—high pressure water jets were directed at the car in a special booth and big fans above blasted and swirled air around it [53]. Other cars were selected for endurance tests on a track (see chapter 9). From November 1963 every second Imp was given a full quality control inspection in a special part of the plant.

A statistical approach was taken to most of the testing. If all went well about thirty per cent of the cars were checked, and if a single fault was found the checks were at once stepped up to one hundred per cent until the trouble was traced and eliminated.

There was no secrecy about faults and their rectification. However carefully assembled cars may be, faults do occur, and the main thing is to find and correct them. Every car had a final inspection on the finish conveyor before going to the customer acceptance department, and another independent inspection there [54]. In addition, quality control could pull any car at random from the line for an

51

52

53

exhaustive re-check in their department, this time on a four-wheel test bed. A percentage of these random cars was also tested on the road for handling, noise and so on. If troubles had been reported with cars in service, the checking was doubled here. Over an inspection pit, all nuts, bolts and vital assemblies were examined for tightness. Suspension and steering geometries were verified and the bodies were filled with smoke to show visually whether the draught sealing was good.

54

After completion, the bodies which had to be stored were sprayed with wax on their upper surfaces for protection against industrial atmospheric fall-out. Completed and tested cars were stored for a period at Linwood until they could be transferred to Coventry.

The now famous 'Imp Special' trains carried 100 cars at a time, and the trains travelled four or five times every day in peak production periods.

It cost approximately £8.10s per car to make this trip, nearly two per cent of the sale price.

55

Having briefly seen the layout of the factory we can move on to the offices, personnel areas and management areas. Firstly after a hard day's work a shower is needed [55]. In addition to the shower baths the amenities block contained a surgery, toilets and locker accommodation. After the shower baths a general view of the self-service works canteen is seen [56] in the personnel block between the unit machine workshop and the die-casting plant.

Moving now into the office block at the front of the factory we first see the main staircase [57] with the receptionist's desk. Ascending to the first landing [58] we find a suite of executive offices such as the one for the accountants on the east wing [59]. The senior executives were well provided for with plush offices [60] and board room [61], where all the managerial decisions were taken. Also of decisive importance must have been the directors' dining room [62, 63] where no doubt many day-to-day problems were thrashed out between senior staff in less formal surroundings. There were two staff restaurants.

The foregoing are the many and varied aspects of building cars for major sale. Everything, from delivery of raw materials to testing and correction of faults must be monitored and controlled. Sophisticated technical and managerial skills were needed to do that and still produce a quality product amenable to the public. Step back from the factory for a moment [64] and visualise this hubbub of fastidious planning which encompassed not only Linwood but also the dealerships whose demand, resulting from publicity and promotion, had to be met by supply here in western Scotland. This is the dream, of smooth production figures sustaining major sales and customer satisfaction from a quality technological product and a job well done. We need, however, also to take into account the labour force, which is the subject of the next chapter.

56

57

58

59

60

61

62

63

4

Meet the Workforce

THE MAIN theme of this book is the activity surrounding production of Hillman Imp cars in the Linwood factory. This production could not have been achieved without the skilled workforce, and we must continually bear in mind the human element in the considerations of production and what is possible in terms of quality and efficiency. Unless you have a keen and settled labour force the job invariably suffers. The Linwood factory was staffed and manned almost entirely by Scots, of whom only a few key personnel were taken to Coventry in the first place for training: the majority were then trained on the job.

The mechanical approach taken by government to restructuring, albeit intended to help alleviate local problems, failed to grasp the underlying difficulties. Industrial relocation is a social process which involves reshaping a series of industrial and economic relations between different companies as well as between management and groups of workers. Neither Pressed Steel nor Rootes fully established links with Scottish enterprise, partly because management was centralised outside the region, and partly because they did not understand the resentment by local firms of new production methods, state assisted wage rates and investment strategies, all of which interfered with their own progress. Much of this resentment later fed through to the workers, causing a series of damaging strikes, with little that government or management could do once the mistakes had been made.

The labour background was Clydesdale shipbuilding and heavy munitions and railway manufacturing both at Pressed Steel Limited and at William Beardmore Limited who preceded them on the Linwood site. Some deep prejudices had to be overcome: for instance, in the past the finishing of a ship usually meant being stood off until new work was found. To work quickly and efficiently was therefore frequently to rush oneself onto the dole. Little wonder that it took time to convince some of the older men and their sons that high productivity in a car plant is to everyone's advantage.

By 1965, after a settling down period the men seemed contented, had built up skills and experience, and were doing a good job. Assuming that the Imp design was at least reasonably good, how did Rootes set about improving both output and quality? Rootes management, under the direction of Bill Garner, in 1966 introduced a 'measured day' incentive work system. They believed that the alternative piecework schemes led to rushed work and reduced quality. They were more concerned with rhythm and constancy of work than with sheer speed.

The scheme worked like this: average factory efficiency according to an agreed non-incentive work study scale, was assessed at a low 75 per cent. The men were then offered an extra 4d an hour on reaching 92 per cent output, another 4d an hour at 96 per cent and 2d at 98 per cent, and a final 2d at 100 per cent. They could thus make an extra 1s an hour on the basic rate—about £2 a week. Management helped in every way it could and production by 1965 was running at 98 per cent. Just for comparison the average take-home pay was around £16 at this time, so the incentives were not negligible.

Flexibility of work, as well as higher productivity, accompanied the improvements and the men were happier because they saw continuity and purpose, and by local standards were now near the top of the league in pay. The company then expected fairly stable conditions and planned on a steady output at fixed rates. They had frankly stated to the press that had Imp costs not come down as pay and productivity went up they would not have been in the business much longer. This was only two years after the initial start of production, and the fine balance of cost and profit continued until the Imp line was abandoned in 1976. The labour force was an all-important factor in the equation of profitability of Linwood and the entire Rootes company. There was little alteration in the labour force from the period of production of only 1,000 cars per week, to that of producing 1,600 better made cars through the incentives, although this figure represented a peak for single-shift production. A new training section was built in 1965 in the original block, which was extended to a second floor for this purpose, again to improve quality and consistency of production.

As well as a large number of men who had experience of working in the shipyards, a section of the workforce consisted of women. In a very professional series of fine photographs we see some of them finishing alloy castings in the machine shop: cleaning the outside edges of hypoid gear casings and drilling the oilways [65], further down the shop the same work continues [66, 67]. Similar work was done in finishing inlet manifolds [68] and drilling crankshaft end bearing caps [69, 70]

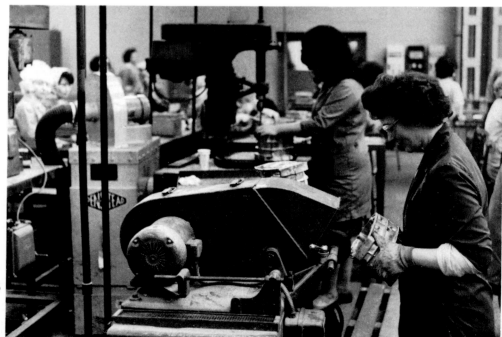

65

66▶

67

68

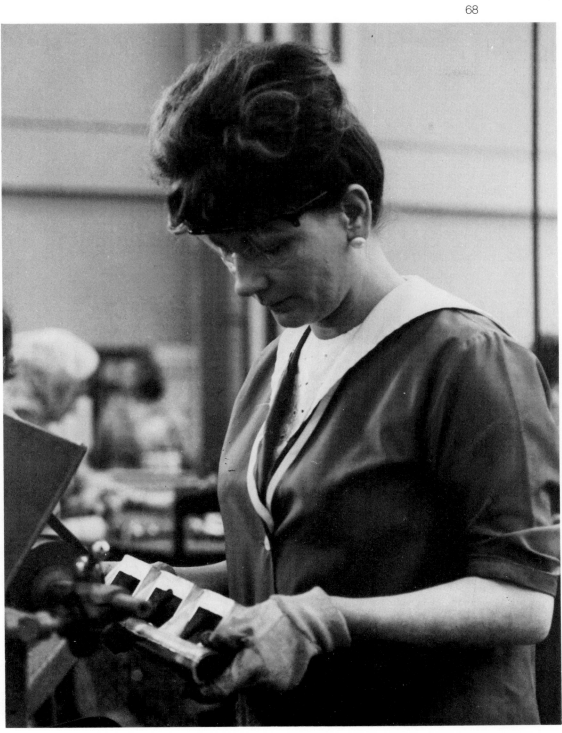

69

70

5

Open Day at Linwood and Family Fun

THE EFFECT of activity around the factory upon the local town of Linwood was considerable. It grew almost as a frontier town, with people arriving daily from Glasgow and the Midlands looking for work and accommodation. Some roads existed only as mud tracks and there were insufficient shops for a population which grew from less than 15,000 to over 22,000 between 1963 and 1966. The local council engaged in a crash house-building programme and promised shops and community facilities to follow. Another aerial view has been augmented by an artist's impression of a new motorway link and high-rise flats [71]. The sprawling mass of new accommodation is seen to the west (lower half of picture 71).

An open day at the factory allowed staff to show their friends and relatives around the place at which they worked. John Queen and W. McNee enthusiastically discuss details of a cutaway section transaxle on display [72]. A. Smith and friends [73] admire the finished and crated Mk 1 engines with their automatic choke units, neatly arranged four per crate for easy transportation. In the same area Mr Hayes gives his family a thorough description of the working of an Imp engine [74]. More senior staff were also at their posts to answer questions. Mr Neil Lucas, of the Sales Department [75] is pictured alongside Imp de Luxe 'IMP 1', as is Mr Graham Hebblethwaite [76] Sales Liaison Executive. Mr J. Cairns and friends [77] take an interest in safety aspects, namely foot brake and handbrake components.

Children are also clearly fascinated by this new car [78], which retailed at only £440 plus £92.4s.7d purchase tax. These were Mr W. Craig's children (goods reviewing department). The car was a de Luxe version, the basic Imp retailed for the lower total price of £508. Tony Samuelle is seen [79] with a group inspecting fully-built up engine and transaxle assemblies, whilst at an earlier stage Mr A. McFadyen and friends guess which cogs are needed for different speeds in the gearbox [80]. A final charming picture shows well-rehearsed children of a senior staff member [81].

Participation of workers in planning was all important, especially when it came to items of clothing for the women! Thus 'Miss Imp' was elected on Tuesday 25 June 1963. A fashion parade for overalls worn by girls from the factory and offices before an appreciative audience of about 300. The factory girls indicated their choice by ballot. The winning overall, worn by Miss Norma Miller, 21, who worked in the die-casting shop, was white with turquoise trimmings [82]. It was later issued to all the girls in the factory.

The Linwood management did all it possibly could to instigate a happy working environment, and the family fun continued with discounted group holidays for the employees. Reproduced here is the original brochure announcing the Continental Motoring Holiday to Switzerland from 18 July to 31 July 1966 [83]. It is not clear whether the employees had to buy an Imp beforehand to benefit from this offer, or if they were only encouraged to consider one after enjoying two weeks of continental motoring! Having driven over a large part of this route myself, I can vouch for the effectiveness of the standard Imp, and also the benefits on hilly terrain of the better braking and increased power output of the Imp Sport. Particularly impressive is the estimated cost of petrol—albeit still as economical as 'DLN 8300' an Imp does not get far on £12 worth today.

71

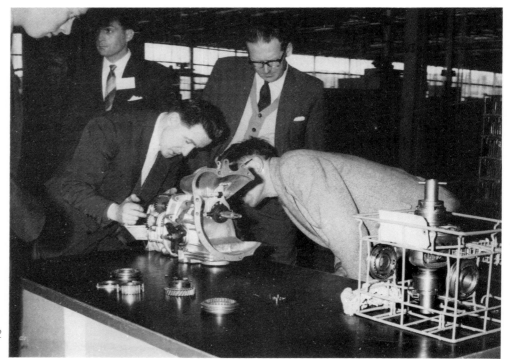

72

73

74

75

76

77

THE NEW
**HILLMAN IMP
DE LUXE SALOON**
£440
£92.4.7.

78

79

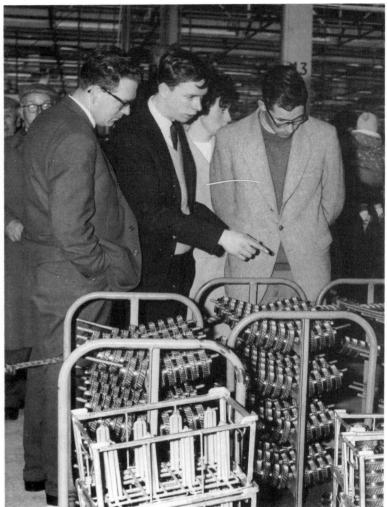

80

81

ROOTES EMPLOYEES'
CONTINENTAL MOTORING HOLIDAY
'SWITZERLAND'

From Monday, July 18th to Sunday, July 31st 1966

THIS COULD BE **YOU** IN YOUR NEW CAR ENJOYING YOUR OWN SPECIAL CONTINENTAL MOTORING HOLIDAY

Try out your car on the traffic-free and scenic Continental roads and give your family a fabulous Swiss holiday on the shores of the picturesque LAKE LUCERNE.

FANTASTIC VALUE FOR MONEY — SPECIAL TERMS APPLICABLE TO THIS UNIQUE HOLI-DAY — ONLY FIRST CLASS ARRANGEMENTS AT MODERATE COST.

SPECIAL ATTRACTIONS include a gay night in BRUSSELS, a visit to the CHAMPAGNE CELLARS and many other excursions and get-togethers. A linguist TOUR MANAGER to take care of all your problems, if any, and to arrange your entertainments — but NO REGIMENTATION, CONVOY DRIVING or 'COACH-PARTY' TREATMENT!

READ THE ITINERARY, SEE ALL THE FACILITIES PROVIDED AND THEN COMPLETE YOUR BOOKING FORM.

ALL FORMALITIES REMOVED, THERE IS NOTHING MORE FOR YOU TO DO, BUT ENJOY THE HOLIDAY!

83

ITINERARY

Monday, 18th July: Dover to Calais — only 1½ hours on the sea. Via Ostend and the new Jabbeke Motorway to BRUSSELS. Dinner at the hotel, then for those who wish an evening in one of the city's gayest nightclubs with excellent cabaret is suggested.

Tuesday, 19th July: Through the Duchy of Luxembourg to EPINAL in the region of the Moselle Valley and Vosges mountains. Dinner at the hotel followed by get-together at the bar.

Wednesday, 20th to Wednesday, 27th July: To Lake Lucerne — WEGGIS. 8 nights at the first class and modern Hotel Alexander on the shores of the lake with its private gardens and lido/bathing beach (see photo). All rooms with bath/shower. Dinner or lunch daily at the hotel. Picnic lunches will be obtainable from the hotel.
Water sports and boating facilities at the lido.

Excursions (individual or party) by steamer to Lucerne, and other lake resorts; by cable car to the mountain peaks of the Rigi, Pilatus and Burgenstock; by car to Zurich, Berne, Susten Pass, Grimsel Pass, etc. ALL ENTIRELY OPTIONAL at popular charges.

Entertainment. Get-togethers, dancing, Swiss evenings, at the hotel and locally. Full details on the spot.

Thursday, 28th July: Through Berne to BIEL on the shores of the lake. Dinner and evening at the hotel.

Friday, 29th July: Via the lake of Neuchatel and Pontarlier to PARCEY. Picturesque setting in the Jura mountains.

Saturday, 30th July: Visit to the Champagne cellars at Epernay with wine tasting, spending the night in Epernay.

Sunday, 31st July: Home, via the Calais/Dover route.

EXAMPLES OF COST PER PERSON

4 persons in Imp   55 gns. per person
3 persons in Imp   56 gns. per person
2 persons in Imp   57 gns. per person
Costs for other Group Models available on request.

CHILDREN CONCESSIONS

For children under 14 years occupying their own rooms at the hotel, the cost will be 38 gns. each.
For children under 14 years occupying their parent's room, further reductions can be obtained to individual requirements.

COST INCLUDES:

1. Transportation of car Dover/Calais return.
2. Passenger tickets return.
3. Port charges and harbour dues.
4. First class hotel accommodation at destination comprising room with bath or shower, dinner or lunch and Continental breakfast. Room, dinner and breakfast en route.
5. Gratuities to hotel servants.
6. Government and local taxes.
7. Road maps, detailed itineraries, town plans.
8. G.B. Plate and Souvenir Plaque/sticker.
9. Services of a linguist Tour Manager.
10. Advice Bulletins covering passports, documentation, petrol and oil, Continental driving conditions with information on road signs, customs regulations, clothing, special diets or dissabilities, insurance, currency — in fact all the information you may need
11. Special insurance scheme at low premiums covering personal accident, medical expenses, loss of baggage, deposit or personal money, all hotel, car hire or travel expenses incurred through a breakdown or accident and towing home of the car to your nearest station.
12. Final Running Schedule giving details of entertainments, names and addresses of hotels, etc. and Passenger List.
13. Various basic entertainments and excursions as mentioned in the itinerary.
14. Documents such as passports will be obtained at cost price.

NOT INCLUDED:

Petrol: Due to the remarkable economy in the fuel consumption of the Imp, this should not be more than about £12 per car.
Pocket Money: Obviously left to personal requirements, depending on the amount of shopping, drinks, etc. you wish to enjoy.
Lunches: Economic picnic lunches or snacks are recommended.

CREDIT FACILITIES

After the initial deposit of £10 per adult sent with the booking form, the remainder can be paid on HP Terms for as little as £4 10. 0. per month (about £1 per week) over a period of 12 months (or 6/9 months) commencing January/February. APPLY FOR APPLICATION FORM WHEN BOOKING.

This is your route —

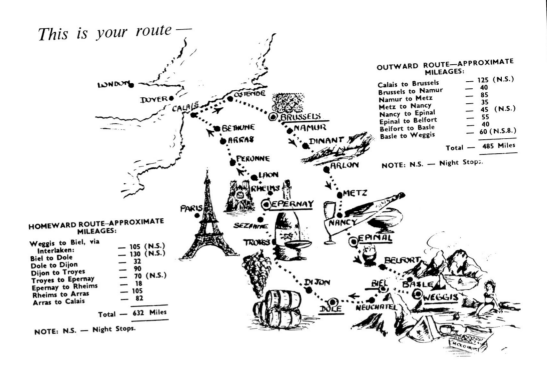

OUTWARD ROUTE—APPROXIMATE MILEAGES:

Calais to Brussels	— 125	(N.S.)
Brussels to Namur	— 40	
Namur to Metz	— 85	
Metz to Nancy	— 35	
Nancy to Epinal	— 45	(N.S.)
Epinal to Belfort	— 55	
Belfort to Basle	— 40	
Basle to Weggis	— 60	(N.S.8.)
Total	— 485 Miles	

NOTE: N.S. — Night Stops.

HOMEWARD ROUTE—APPROXIMATE MILEAGES:

Weggis to Biel, via Interlaken:	— 105	(N.S.)
Biel to Dole	— 130	(N.S.)
Dole to Dijon	— 32	
Dijon to Troyes	— 90	
Troyes to Epernay	— 70	(N.S.)
Epernay to Rheims	— 18	
Rheims to Arras	— 105	
Arras to Calais	— 82	
Total	— 632 Miles	

NOTE: N.S. — Night Stops.

This is your Hotel —

ROOTES EMPLOYEES'
CONTINENTAL MOTORING HOLIDAY 'SWITZERLAND'
BOOKING FORM

To : Group Accredited Motor Touring Agents
Continental Touring Club Ltd., 11 Bathurst Street, London, W.2.
Telephone : AMBassador 1367 & 9871.

Subject to accommodation being available please book me on Continental motoring Holiday 'Switzerland'

.... Make of car .... Model ....

H.P./CC. .... Year of make .... Registration No. ....

I am/am not a member of A.A./R.A.C. .... Membership No. ....
(Please state which)

There will be .... persons in my party and we shall require hotel accommodation consisting of :—
.... single rooms (with/without bath) and .... double rooms (Large bed/twin beds)
(with/without private bathrooms).

I enclose cash/cheque/money order value £... being a deposit of £10 per person (adult).
Cheques/Money Orders should be crossed and made payable to Continental Touring Club Ltd. Upon completion of reservations I will forward the balance of cost upon receipt of your invoice. I accept the conditions as printed overleaf.

BLOCK CAPITALS PLEASE

NAME ....

ADDRESS ....

Telephone No. .... (between 9 a.m. and 6 p.m.) Telephone No. .... (other times)

.... Signature

It is essential that this questionnaire be completed in respect of each member of the party.

A Mr. Mrs., Miss	B SURNAME	C FULL CHRISTIAN NAMES	D DATE OF BIRTH	E PASSPORT NUMBER	F DATE OF ISSUE

NOTE.— If any member of the party is not in possession of a passport, please insert the word "wanted" in column 'E' and the necessary application forms will be sent at once. If passport is being issued but the number is not available, please insert in column 'E' the words " to follow " and advise the passport number and date of issue as quickly as possible.

CREDIT FACILITIES:—I*do/do not wish to avail myself of HP terms spread over *6 months/9 months/12 months.
*Delete where inapplicable.

CONDITIONS OF BOOKING

CONTINENTAL TOURING CLUB LIMITED hereby give notice that in making the arrangements for which tickets and/or vouchers have been issued to the Passenger, they have done so only as Agents, and that all such arrangements are made on the following terms and conditions:

(1) The service provided by the Company is subject to the laws of the country in which such service is provided and the passenger will be responsible for compliance with such laws

(2) The Company do not accept any liability for any loss or expense that may be incurred by the Passenger attributable to (a) delays from any cause whatsoever in any train or steamer or air services or by reason of cancellation of any such service; (b) any accident, injury, loss or damage that may be suffered by the Passenger in any way arising out of the service provided to the Passenger by the Company.

(3) The Company do not accept any liability in respect of any luggage or effects belonging to the Passenger and the Passenger will be responsible for compliance with all requirements of the Customs Authorities in relation thereto. The Passenger will be responsible for all articles other than luggage, including hand-bags, wearing apparel, umbrellas, etc

(4) The Company reserves the right to withdraw or modify the arrangements made with the Passenger in whole or in part and any increased charge made by any operating Company or body will fall upon the Passenger. In the event of the arrangements being completely

withdrawn the Company will refund to the Passenger any deposit the Passenger may have paid and on such refund the Company shall not be under any other liability to the Passenger.

(5) In the event of cancellation of a holiday or booking by the client, the following shall apply:—

(a) In the case of Rallies or full independent tours, the Company shall be entitled to retain the booking fee and recover from the client any expenses incurred in connection with the booking such as cancellation fees, etc.

(b) In the case of Transportation tickets the company will obtain refunds from the carrier concerned, but the client will remain responsibile for the cost until any refund obtainable is credited to the Company by the conveyor concerned. N.B. Refunds often take several months to obtain.

(6) If payment is made by cheque, a receipt will not be sent unless specifically requested. The Company will accept the paid cheque as evidence of payment.

(7) Changes in International exchange carrying increased costs to the Company will be borne by the passenger

6

The V.I.P Treatment

NOT ONLY did the employees get the VIP treatment on special occasions, but they were able to show off their skills to other visitors. Especially entertaining is the 'visit to Rootes (Scotland) Limited, on Wednesday 5 June 1963, of Mr E. F. McBride, 101 Greenhead Street, Bridgetown, Glasgow. Mr McBride was 77 years old and was trained with the old Scottish Argyll Motor Company at their Hosier Street works in Glasgow. He held a Glasgow driving licence number 513, issued in 1903. Mr Anderson, Rootes driver at Linwood, holds open the door for Mr McBride to enter the Hillman Imp from his Greenhead Street home at 9.30 a.m. [84]. Mr McBride is seen being welcomed by Mr W. F. C. Bryant, Director and General Manager of Rootes (Scotland) Limited, at approximately 10.15 a.m. at Rootes Linwood [85]. In the centre is Mr Graham Hebblethwaite, Sales Liaison Executive, Linwood. Next Mr Hebblethwaite, Mr McBride, Mr Neil Lucas and Mr Bryant discuss differences between production standards of 1903 and 1963 in the Linwood showroom [86].

"Mr. Andrew McBride 77, was making cars in Scotland 60 years ago. Argyll Voiturettes, turned out by the Hosier Engineering Company, of Bridgetown. The factory had a staff of 20 and made one car a week. The Argyll had a 3 hp engine, weighed 4½ cwt, cruised at 12 miles an hour on the level—and cost £115, which was worth £900 now (in 1963). Mr. McBride listened quietly as he was told that the Linwood factory already employs 2,000 people and will eventually make 3,000 cars a week. He admired the finer points of the Imp's engine—the world's newest. He was impressed by the Imp's power and performance, but it was the hundreds of girls assembling components which really caught his eye. 'Changed days' he said, 'a wee lassie can now build a modern car. It's a braw car'." [87]

This mythical figure of 3,000 cars a week was often quoted in press releases, but was of course never achieved and caused a lot of trouble. Die-casting capabilities were simply not able to go much above 1,500 cars a week. Although more than in 1903, this was a very low figure from a modern nineteen-sixties specially-built factory, but was all that could be expected from a single shift. Even by 1974 with easier-to-build Hillman Hunters also being assembled at Linwood, production rarely exceeded 2,000 on a single shift.

"Mr. McBride commenting on 'slight' engine differences from the 1903 Argyll and 1963 Imp, with Mr. Neil Lucas." [88, 89] They are looking at a completely assembled engine prior to fitting to a car. "Mr. Graham Hebblethwaite introduces

84

85

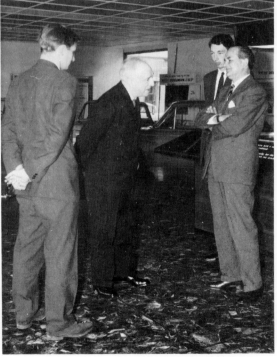

86

87

88

89

90

91

92

93

Mr. McBride to Mr. Charles Braidwood a foreman on the assembly line, whose father also built Argyll cars in the Alexandria works some 50 years ago [90]. Mr. McBride recalls with Miss Joyce Ritchie and Mr. Graham Hebblethwaite, the days when, at Hosier Street in 1903, only one girl looked after the upholstery of the Argyll cars [91].

"Introduced by Mr. Graham Hebblethwaite, Mr. McBride (77 – retired some 12 years) talks with Mr. Alex Wise (72 – and currently test driver with Rootes Linwood) the pros and cons of the Argyll car on which Mr. McBride served his time against the Arrol-Johnson on which Mr. Alex Wise served his time." [92] Incidentally Alex Wise started his apprenticeship in 1908, and became test driver for Arrol-Johnson: he drove one of the three Arrol-Johnsons entered for the 1912 French Grand Prix and achieved fifth place. He retired officially from the plant in Coventry, but volunteered his services as a test driver when Rootes moved to Scotland in 1962. He was thus able to drive the famous 100,000 test car 'WHS 171', a red Imp depicted, with Mr Wise at the wheel, in the Henshaws' book. Mr McBride is driven by Mr Graham Hebblethwaite in a new Imp from the end of the production line [93].

"Miss Sandra Bloom, Mr. McBride and Miss Eva Richter find some social significance between the speed of the new Imp and current day boys." [sic] [94] Interestingly they are standing behind the cutaway engine in the showroom at Linwood—highly polished and prepared in order to show the internal workings to visitors. "Mr. Graham Hebblethwaite, Mr. McBride and Mr. W. F. C. Bryant take serious thought on the past and future of the Scottish Motor Industry [95].

94

95

96

Mr. McBride shakes hands with Mr. Bryant, at the end of an interesting morning's visit to the Rootes factory at Linwood." [96]

It is certain that there must have been a lot of local interest in the activities of Rootes, and that the effect on the local population and industry was potentially very large. The Rootes company were clearly interested to have good relations with all parties: having a good reputation means that the workforce will take a pride in the company and thus make their best effort. The advantage which accrued from having good public relations is not as obvious as the increase in sales through advertising, but it is nonetheless important. The local population was therefore shown first-hand just how clean, safe and well organised was the Linwood site.

Indeed so important was it to promote the good name of Linwood that the site was blessed with a visit of the Moderator of the General Assembly of the Church of Scotland, the Rt. Reverend James S. Stewart BD [97]. We see the party standing beneath the overhead transporter track [98], from left to right: Reverend A.

97   98

Ralston, D. G. N. Hannay (Company Secretary), Reverend Dr W. H. Rogan, Rt. Reverend James S. Stewart BD and E. Minton (Supervisor of the car assembly building). Next we see the party inspecting an Imp which has reached the end of the assembly track and is almost ready to be driven off [99]. Front row: E. Minton and the Moderator, Rt. Reverend James S. Stewart BD. Back row: Reverend Dr W. H. Rogan, D. G. N. Hannay, Reverend E. R. Marr, Reverend A. Ralston, Reverend W. W. M. Bell, and Reverend R. C. M. Morton.

As well as the clergy other influential dignitaries visited the plant. One was the Rt. Hon. Lord Craighton CBE, PC, Minister of State for Scotland, who came to Linwood on 26 September 1963 to be taken on a tour of the factory by the Hon. Geoffrey Rootes [100]. He examined a Hillman Imp engine both before [101] and after [102] installation in the car. Again the former engine in question is the show engine. Movement of the internal parts can be appreciated through the cutaway sections in the engine, transaxle and ancillary components such as the fuel pump and carburettor automatic choke and air filter housing. The crankshaft would be turned slowly by an electric motor placed under the display stand and protected from stray fingers by a polished metal casing at the front. Perspex covers protect other delicate parts (of the engine, not the anatomy).

99

100

After further discussion with Geoffrey Rootes on the subject of car production, Lord Craighton was shown the interior of a finished Imp [103] and then drove another slightly less finished example within the factory [104].

t>

101

102

103

104

Another very important visitor who came to see the Rootes Group factory at Linwood during his visit to Glasgow on 24 February 1964 was the then Prime Minister, the Rt. Hon. Sir Alec Douglas-Home. The picture [105] shows the Prime Minister inspecting the Hillman Imp during his tour of the assembly shop.

105

7

Exhibition for Scottish Industry, 1963

WE WILL take a break from the tours and look a little more at the involvement of local industry in the Linwood project. An exhibition for Scottish companies was held in the foyer and showroom of the factory from 3 to 13 September 1963. This exhibition was meant to emphasise the indirect benefits to employment in the area by the use of locally-produced bought-in components as well as directly in the assembly work. Of course the Pressed Steel company featured strongly in this since they employed as many people as the main Linwood site did in producing the Imp bodyshell. The first picture [106] shows Mr Neil Lucas of Rootes showing visitor Mr Dunlop the good ergonomics of the Imp. The second picture [107] is of Mr B. O. Massey (Chief Buyer, Rootes (Scotland) Limited), Hector Stevenson (Industrial Correspondent with the *Evening Citizen*), and Andrew Hargrave (a freelance journalist). Also on display were various components of the Hillman Imp which were bought from sources outside the Rootes and Pressed Steel companies [108]. The exhibition was open to potential and existing suppliers [109, 110]. It was partly organised by Linwood Managing Director, G. H. B. Cattell, and he maintained that it was necessary to fulfil the pledge to promote industrial development in Scotland.

Ideally, for company strategy, Rootes Linwood should have become self-sufficient. There were four main units (as explained in Chapter 3); the die-casting plant, the machine and assembly shops for mechanical units and, across the road under the direction of Peter Griffiths, Rootes Pressings, formerly Pressed Steel. Rootes Pressings made the bodies and delivered them, painted, trimmed and ready for assembly, by overhead conveyor. The engines were built in Coventry and delivered to the unit assembly section. Self-sufficiency would have called for a Scottish engine plant.

A few components continued to be bought in—wheels and tyres from Dunlop and Goodyear (and earlier India Rubber Limited in Inchinnan), fuel tanks from Rubery Owen (who opened a new factory at Cumbernauld in Scotland), suspension wishbones from Sankey Wellington, clutch assemblies from Laycock, and crankshafts via Coventry from Ambrose Shardlow in Hartlepool. Steering racks came from manufacturers Cam Gears Limited. The only casting not handled by the new die-casting plant at Linwood was the difficult cylinder head from Aeroplane and Motor Aluminium Castings in Birmingham. Rootes were, however, exceptional in making their own radiators and heaters in a special section alongside the main assembly line. Self-sufficiency was not, however, what the politicians had in mind in inviting Rootes to Scotland.

Undoubtedly Rootes were not just window-shopping in 1963, having already taken the plunge into the Clyde valley. Scottish firms were shown all the bought-in parts down to details and were invited to tender for them: £10 million worth of orders were available, but very few could handle the work or quote competitive prices. Of 600 companies who sent representatives to Linwood, 400 submitted quotes but of these only 15 were given immediate contracts. It was also not viable for many English ancillary firms to open north of the border for two reasons: they already had sufficient capacity and also subcontracted to smaller firms in the Midlands. They were, in addition, easily able to undercut Scottish companies by offering package deals to Rootes. The indigenous managers were furthermore wary of being dominated by the giant newcomer who, in their eyes, did not promise a secure future—such being the time scales of operation and conservatism in Scotland!

An example of the failure of the exhibition is of a local manufacturer who tendered for a component in high grade steel. The units were offered at 3½d as a loss leader, but this price was still undercut by a Midlands supplier at £1 per gross. The latter concern made a 100% loss, but offered several other components which required re-tooling: these absorbed the cost.

106

The Labour Opposition stridently criticised the MacMillan Government for their relocation policy. Dr Dickson Mabon, then Labour MP for Greenock, raised the issue of secondary employment creation in the important Commons debate of Scotland (Industry and Employment) in July 1962: "...we are told that the arrival of the Rootes factory will solve all the difficulties of the county of Renfrew. On the record of experience at Bathgate [where BMC had been given money to build cars, but built tractors instead], this is just not true. The Government so far are failing to attract the industries ancillary and subsidiary to these large factories to Scotland. They ought to be large industrial complexes attracting more industries and more jobs than the main factories themselves represent." [ref. 7]

107

108

The regional policy followed by the Government was sadly deficient in building bridges between indigenous and migrant firms, and in providing capital to enable firms to compete with established ancillary suppliers. Subcontracts are part of the growth of any new industry, almost as important as the industry itself and the Government was much criticised by local as well as opposition MPs. This controversy did not help sell the Imp.

All the same, Geoffrey Rootes was able to tell Sir Alec Douglas-Home during his visit to the plant in February 1964 that the Scottish content of the cars was 76 per cent.

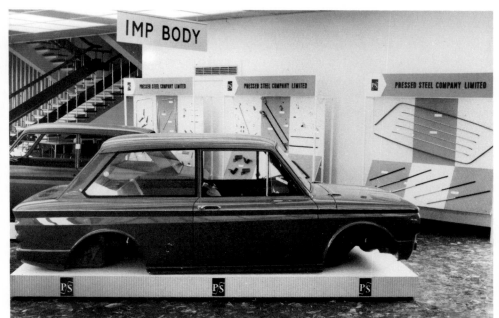

109

110

8

MPs Tour Imp Factory at Linwood

IN CHAPTER 6 the readiness was noticed with which Rootes (Scotland) Limited received visitors, albeit exceptional ones, and the very likely importance which this must have had for promoting a smoothly running business with good public acceptance both locally and nationally. This continued throughout the early years.

"The contribution of the British Motor Industry in setting up new factories in depressed areas will be seen by 38 Conservative and Labour MPs on Wednesday (3 July 1963).

"Under arrangements made by the Society of Motor Manufacturers and Traders, the MPs will see two motor factories in Scotland, one being the new Rootes plant at Linwood, near Glasgow, where the Hillman Imp is made.

"The visits are considered to be of political importance, because of the emphasis on the Motor Industry's steps to relieve unemployment.

"At Linwood MPs will be shown the working of one of the most modern car manufacturing plants in Europe, and will see the production of the first British car to be made in Scotland for over 30 years.

"The Hillman Imp embodies many imaginative features. It is, for example, the first British car in large-scale production to have an aluminium die-cast engine, which is largely responsible for its exceptional performance and economy. Such features have attracted very great interest—and very large orders—from many countries. These in turn naturally represent work and jobs for the Scottish factory.

"They will be escorted round the factory by the Hon. Geoffrey Rootes, Chairman of Rootes (Scotland) Ltd., and they will meet some of the 2,000 workers. Ultimately the factory will employ 5,000 people."

We start with the Hon. Geoffrey Rootes again explaining the functionality of the factory and giving an overview to the entire group [111, 112]. He then shows them the product and the actual factory. Firstly in the showroom at the front of the main building a smaller group sees the show car 'IMP 1', and praises the neat layout of the engine compartment [113 see front jacket/cover]. After this a larger group of visitors pro-gresses to the assembly plant where transaxle casings attract great interest. The extreme lightness of these alloy castings is something exceptional. It is possible to lift them with just a little finger [114] or even throw them in the air [115]!

111

112

(113: See front jacket/cover)

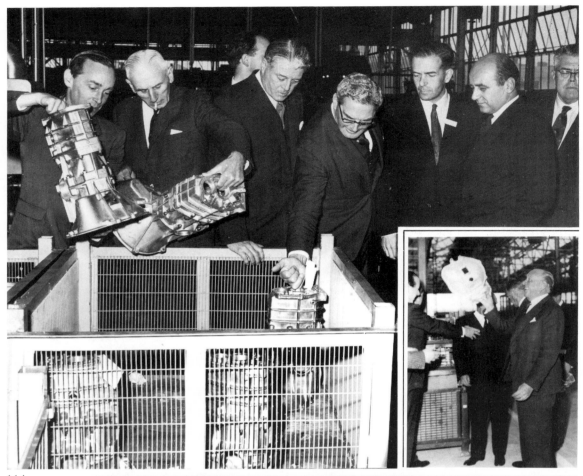

114

115 (inset)

116

117

118

Completed transaxle units (considerably heavier once their steel gears had been installed) are bolted onto the engine and rear suspension, as demonstrated by one of the assembly workers [116, 117]. Another explains the same procedure to— from left to right—M. J. Prior, Conservative MP Lowestoft; George Kane, Rootes (Scotland) Limited; W. F. C. Bryant, Manager and Director of Rootes (Scotland) Limited); R. Gresham Cooke CBE, Conservative MP Twickenham [118].

Geoffrey Rootes himself explains some of the manufacturing process to a charming female visitor in the same group (her name is not recorded) [119].

Rootes continues his explanations as the tour proceeds around the factory [120], with questions and answers freely flowing [121, 122]. He discusses an aspect of local Scottish interest with Tam Dalyell, Labour MP for West Lothian [123, 124]. Note that this visit chronologically preceded the exhibition of the last chapter and there was concern at this time for more local involvement in the production (following the Commons debate on Industry and Employment in Scotland in July 1962).

Other members of the group see for themselves work carried out on the Imp bodyshell before it is dropped onto the rear suspension assembly [125].

The MPs who visited the factory of course represented the political machine which had brought it into being, and were probably aware of the key importance of it in the British employment and export policy which had been pursued for nearly two decades. They had come to see at first hand the results of this policy, and were undoubtedly very impressed. Nevertheless the insertion of an established English industry which had its headquarters in the Midlands into distant mid-western Scotland created stress and did not result in the anticipated large local expansion. It would have been economically unfeasible for Rootes or Pressed Steel to use land in Scotland without considerable Government investment, and this artificial situation could not be maintained. This has been shown time and time again thoughout the history of Linwood since the war years when the site was a Ministry of Supply shadow factory for the production of munitions under the local company of William Beardmore Limited.

It was understandable that the Ministry of Employment wanted to maintain employment of the population who had been involved in this, and also the factory site, and moreover to relieve the growing unemployment in the area by redistributing jobs from the Midlands where labour was scarce. In 1946 the Scottish regional section of the Ministry of Labour produced a document entitled *Full Employment Policy – Motor Car Industry in Scotland* [ref. 2] which attracted attention to the massive male labour surplus of 60,000 in the Glasgow, Greenock and Port Glasgow areas. The 1945 'Distribution of Industry Act' enabled action to be taken.

Similar policies were common practice in other countries at the time. Perhaps with hindsight we can say that this was not successful. Firstly a large amount of national expenditure was needed to persuade industry into the area; secondly there was a complex interaction with local economics. There was no plan as to how the new companies and the established companies should co-exist. There was no study of the need for the English and Scottish branches of Rootes to maintain wage parity, with the result that existing Scottish companies had then to offer similar wages. This led to much unrest of the labour force. There was also no clear plan to improve local amenities, as is witnessed by the uncontrolled growth of Linwood town.

119

120

121

122 ◀ 123 ▶

124

125

9

Track Record

WITH THE increasing success of the Imp, testing and production did not stop. Indeed the early test phases has been characterised by their exhaustive long-distance, speed and endurance aspects (see the Henshaws' book). This continued with tests of finished cars both in the Linwood factory and on the track. A large number of works cars were used for this purpose: seen here are Coventry registered '802 KV' and '4406 KV' undergoing endurance tests. Note the single spot lamp on '4406 KV' for continuous night and day driving. [126-127].

Many of these 'works' cars were sold cheaply after about a year to private motor clubs who would use them, after a little modification, in competition. There were, however, not many genuine 'works competition' cars, and the distinction is at first sight difficult to make since they mostly carried Coventry registrations.

A small sample of the original test documentation is reproduced in the following pages. It is rather technical but gives a glimpse at the thoroughness of the Rootes approach to the motor industry. The cars and ½- and ¼-scale models were subjected to wind-tunnel tests at the famous MIRA test centre. The ¼-scale model Imp is indeed still preserved at MIRA [128-130]. Some results are shown which are relevant to circulation of air around the Imp saloon body. The company was particularly concerned that the through-flow air system, a unique feature of the early Imps, might not operate correctly because of possible poor assembly of the body panels or wear of the seals while in use. Exhaust fumes had been found to enter the car, endangering the occupants, and the source of this worry was investigated. This information should also be of interest to present-day owners who do long-distance driving [131].

A further concern was for the cooling performance of the rear radiator and fan. A minimalist approach had been used to its initial design and the radiator was barely adequate when new. This concept of marginal cooling came from the Ryton design office, but was never fully developed, partly because the small team there was separated from the larger, more experienced, team in Stoke. To add insult to injury some of the 4 psi pressure radiator caps which had been specified for the production were found to leak, and the specification was uprated to include 7 psi caps (as fitted up until 1976). This, however, to some extent aggravated the problem as now the gland seals on the Mk 1 water pump could not withstand the extra pressure. Today, restored cars can be fitted with improved radiators, and later Sport models had slots cut in the engine compartment lid as

126

127

128

129

130

RCT/TRC/GMA.
9.9.64. CONFIDENTIAL

EXPERIMENTAL DEPT.
REPORT

Report No.	3062.
Date	31.8.64.
Model Project No.	2850.
Sub-Project No.	
Phase	
T.R. No.	LTD/743.
T.R. Category.	
X.A. No.	

File Ref: B.2. Imp.

TO   Mr. L. Kuzmicki.   (2).

MODEL   Imp Saloon.   VEHICLE   MILEAGE

SUBJECT.   SECTION I.
Exhaust Fume Entry.

AIM.
To trace the path of exhaust fume entry on Imp Saloon.

CONCLUSIONS.
Exhaust Fumes were found to enter the body in the following places in order of severity.

1. Backlight lock.
2. Rear Air Extractors above backlight.
3. Backlight surround - rubber seal.
4. Door seals on lower edge.
5. Heater intake.

The region of the backlight and surround is in a relatively higher pressure zone than the car interior, particularly when the quarter vent windows are open, therefore, if the opening backlight is not well sealed or the none return flaps do not seal properly then exhaust fumes will be sucked in.

When the car is rapidly slowed down to walking pace then there is a tendency for exhaust fumes to be drawn forward, caused mainly by the forward flow of the Engine Cooling Fan, particularly if there is a side wind. The result of this is to suck exhaust fumes in through the lower door seals, if the door seals are poor and the quarter vents are open, also a small quantity of exhaust fumes may enter the Heater Intakes.

RECOMMENDATIONS.

1. The sealing of the backlight lock and rubber seal should be improved.
2. The rubber flaps on the air extractors should be improved or the extractors resited to a more efficient location.
3. Door sealing to be improved.
4. Heater intake resited to scuttle area.
5. Change Fan to reverse flow or duct engine cooling air out rearward.

STATE OF T.R.
T.R. LDT/743 is now closed.

Circulation.

Mr. P. G. Ware.	All.			
Mr. T. L. Jump.	Sec.1.			
Mr. D. Hodkin.	"			
Mr. P. S. Wilson.	All.			
Mr. D. R. Welbourne.	"			
Mr. E. F. Litchfield.	Sec.1.			
Mr. V. J. Adrian.	"			
Mr. F. J. Smithyman.	"			
Mr. W. T. Oliver.	All.			
Mr. P. M. T. Cobley.	"	Mr. R. L. Croft.	All.)	
Mr. P. J. Nevitt. (2)	"	Mr. K. M. Davis.	")	
Mr. L. T. Price.	Sec.1.	Mr. F. B. Evans.	")	Ryton.
Mr. K. W. Sharpe.	All.	Mr. H. W. White.	")	
Mr. H. Sharon.	Sec.1.	Mr. F. D. Marsden.	")	
Mr. F. A. Coine.	All.	Mr. R. C. Tustin.	"	
Mr. C. W. Mann.	"	Mr. T. R. Carpenter.	"	

REPORTED BY. ....
AIRFLOW ENGINEER.

APPROVED BY ....
DYNAMICS ENGINEER.

TRC/RTC/GMA.
9.9.64.

REPORT NO. 3062

SECTION II.

DESCRIPTION OF TEST.

     The test was carried out on an Imp vehicle in the M.I.R.A. Wind Tunnel to determine the path of exhaust fume entry. Smoke was used emitted near to the exhaust pipe and around the likely places of entry into the body.

RESULTS AND CONCLUSIONS.

     The worst condition was found to be, heater closed and vent windows open, when the car is slowed down rapidly.

     The vent windows being open create a depression inside the car which sucks the exhaust fumes in.

     Leaks occurred in the following places in order of severity.

    I. Opening back light lock.

    2. Rear air extractors.

    3. Backlight surround - rubber seal.

    4. Door seals on lower edge.

    5. Front heater intake.

     A larger flow of smoke could be detected passing through the backlight lock.

     The none-return flaps on the rear air extractors were not functioning correctly. These extractors are wrongly positioned to effect extraction (see Report 2642). It was noticed that the engine cooling fan sucked the exhaust smoke forward, which brought the exhaust fumes in close contact with the lower edge of the doors and the heater intakes when the car speed is reduced quickly.

Reported by. *[signature]*
T. R. CARPENTER.

---

indicated in this report [132]. The water pump was remodelled for the Mk 2 cars. Other novel ideas to come from Ryton which were originally fitted but later dropped from the production cars in early 1965 included the automatic choke, and pneumatic throttle linkage. Another study was made of gearbox cooling, which had caused problems at high speeds. No action was taken, however, for cooling was not a real problem during normal motoring, provided that the oil level in the transaxle was maintained at its correct level.

RGT/TRC/JMH   CONFIDENTIAL   26 JUN 1964 | Report No.   2722

11-6-64   **EXPERIMENTAL DEPT.** | Date   1596-04

                REPORT | Model Project No.

                                                           | Sub-Project No.

File: B.2 Imp | Phase

                                                           | T.R. No.   LTD.659

TO   MR. K. W. SHARPE (2)

MODEL	IMP SALOON	VEHICLE	MILEAGE

SECTION I

SUBJECT - WIND TUNNEL TESTS

AIM

1) To investigate position for a scuttle heater air intake.
2) To obtain pressure distribution over rear end with reverse flow engine cooling fan, together with combinations of deflectors or scoops under the car with louvres and slots in the top and rear of the engine compartment lid.
3) Investigate effect of gearbox cooling air intake and engine compartment louvres on aerodyanamic coefficients.

CONCLUSIONS

1) The best position for a scuttle air intake would be immediately in front of the windscreen base on the centre line of car, and should not be more than 12" wide.

   The pressure coefficient on the rear of the luggage compartment lid was only 75% of that on the scuttle. Therefore in terms of airflow, the scuttle air intake would deliver at least twice the airflow of that delivered through the location in the rear of the luggage compartment lid.

2) The original slots in the engine compartment lid extract air with the fan giving a reverse flow to normal. The lower slots which are in line with the rear number plate extract air, and the airflow is unaffected when the original slots are blanked.

   The louvres in the top of the engine compartment lid extract air, but there is little change in total air extracted by placing the louvres forwards, rearwards, inside or outside, but the proportion of airflow out of the louvres to out of the rear slots will   depend   upon the direction of the louvres.

   When the spoilers or vanes are fitted on the rear suspension arms, then more air is extracted through the louvres and less through the rear slots, but if the gearbox scoop is used, then the airflow is increased through the rear slots and reduced through the louvres.

   The louvres have virtually no effect on the drag coefficient Cd, but the vanes on the suspension arms increase the Cd by .01 compared with the gearbox scoop.

RECOMMENDATIONS

That the rear slots and louvres be incorporated into the engine compartment lid to improve the airflow. The actual direction of the louvres can be selected by styling as this has little effect on the airflow.

Bandu
W.P.C. M.4425
Form 1612C

Cont'd...

- 2 -

RCT/TRC/JMH   Report No.2799
11-6-64   TR.No. LTD.659

    The gearbox scoop to be fitted to give increased airflow through engine compartment and lower Cd than with spoilers on suspension arms, although spoilers may deflect more air over the actual gearbox but reduce airflow through the whole engine compartment and increase drag.

STATE OF TR.

    TR. LTD.659 is now closed.

Reported by ....
                      AIRFLOW ENGINEER

Approved by ....
                      DYNAMICS ENGINEER

Circulation:

Mr. P. G. Ware	Sect.1
Mr. T. L. Jump	Sect.1
Mr. D. Hodkin	Sect.1
Mr. P. S. Wilson	All
Mr. D. R. Welbourne	All
Mr. E. F. Litchfield	Sect.1
Mr. V. J. Adrian	Sect.1
Mr. F. J. Smithyman	Sect.1
Mr. W. T. Oliver	All
Mr. P. M. T. Cobley	All
Mr. P. J. Nevitt	All + Sec.1
Mr. L. T. Price	Sect.1
Mr. L. Kuzmicki (2)	All
Mr. D. W. Brummitt	Sect.1
Mr. C. W. Mann)	All
Mr. R. L. Croft)	All
Mr. K. M. Davis) Ryton	All
Mr. F. B. Evans)	All
Mr. H. W. White)	All
Mr. M. Rushall)	All
Mr. E. S. White) Eng.	Sect.1
Mr. T. G. R. Fleming) Studio	Sect.1
Mr. R. C. Tustin	All
Mr. T. R. Carpenter	All

10

How These Imps Are Really Made!

FIVE SHOTS of a half-built Imp shell on the Pressed Steel factory production line are shown. These photographs are of exceptional quality and details of the body welding around the inner wing, chassis rail and floor area can easily be seen [133], and also the interior construction of the floor pan, rear seat section, door pillars and completed sill [134]. This car is ready to have wings and front panel installed, and one shell in more advanced state is seen in the next picture [135]. The details of the railway-style wagons which held and transported the Imp shells are also evident. These were part of the manufacturing chain and important tools in the production process.

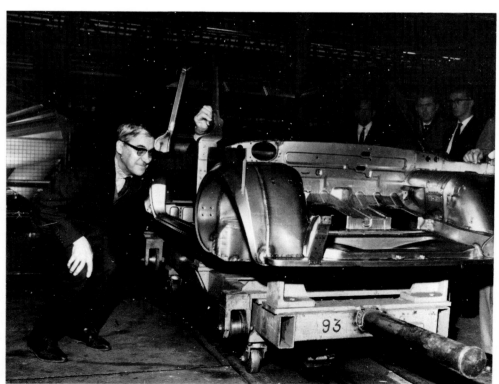

133

134

135

Newly painted Imp shells in primer [136] prior to receiving miraculous mirror finish top paint coats [137].

136

137

The product takes shape on the assembly line where final components are added. Access could be gained from the sides, front and underside of the vehicle by both workers and visitors alike [138]. The car depicted here has no lights, wheels or any other main items of trim. Further down the line a nearly completed example has its bumpers, wheels and trim fitted. It has been lowered onto its wheels but still has protective bandaging on the chrome work [139]. It is possible to sit in the car to see the ergonomic layout of the interior and appreciate the quality of the seating. The interior of an Imp was much more comfortable and less spartan than that of other small cars of the period. The Imp also had many original features such as electro-magnetic indicator controls, and luxury fittings in common with the rest of the Rootes range, such as wind-up windows.

138

140

139

141

This completed car took shape in the form of 'VHS 813' and would have been driven off the end of the production line into the test area [140-143]. When the car had passed scrutineering it was driven out of the factory into the parking lot [144]. Even at this time the isolated nature of Linwood is apparent, with the Scottish hills in the distance and a journey of 14 miles necessary to reach the night life of Glasgow.

142

143

144

11

Flights to the Imps

WITH GROWING awareness and market for the new Imp over the next year the publicity exercise took off!

"Transport managers and other senior executives from some of Britain's biggest industrial and commercial organisations flew from London to Scotland in a chartered Viscount to visit the Linwood factory. The party included representatives of the North Thames Gas Board which operates a fleet of 112 Imps. 'They were all very impressed with what they saw', said Mr M. K. Brown, manager, fleet sales department. The photograph shows the party disembarking at Renfrew Airport, 16/4/64." [145] "So many Rootes dealers wanted to visit the company's Scottish factory, where Hillman Imps were produced at a rate of 2,000 a week, that the 60-seat turbo-prop Viscount airliner was chartered on a regular basis by the group for a series of six flights from various airports in England and Wales." [146] As usual the tour of inspection started with an overview of the factory layout; this time, however, Lord Rootes is absent and another member of the senior staff takes the helm [147].

145

146

147

As well as the North Thames Gas Board many other companies used Imps for their business. One example was the Granada TV Rental Company, who used fleets of Hillman Huskies from 1968 to around 1973. They were mainly painted forest green, but the later ones were accepted in all colours, much to the delight of the employees. The huskies were modified to suit the company's needs, the main difference being mounting holes near the rear of the side windows into which supports for advertising boards could be placed. The front support was caught in the window runner to keep the whole thing securely in place on the sides of the vehicle, so that the overall effect was that of a small van with the usual windows obscured. Hillman Huskies were the cheapest vehicle which could serve the purpose, being sufficiently roomy to accommodate the large new colour televisions of the time, unlike their competitors which could not. A side effect of having the rear engine was that the heat kept the electronics dry. So successful were these huskies that I know of people in the TV repair business who have kept them to this day for their work!

In the unit machine workshop the 1964 group of transport executives inspect some of the accurate machining work carried out on the transaxle housing [148, 149], in this illustration the hypoid casing. These casing components are worthy of note [150]. Their production from aluminium alloy by the pressure die-casting process makes them light and strong. The accurate machining and assembly is essential to correct and reliable working of the transaxle. The good feel and quick

148

149

150

151

152

153

154

155

156

gearchange for which the Imp is renowned results from the original design, a complete remodelling of the Villiers unit studied in the early prototype car. The design also provided for correct assembly procedures to be implemented, as seen here. Other components for the gearbox emerge from the special Churchill machine where they are cut and assembled [151, 152], these being the main driveshafts and gears. Differential crown wheels [153] are put together with the rest of their components and assembled into the transaxle under careful guidance on a special jig [154].

The unit workshop also produced the finished rear suspension trailing arms, using the Archdale Transfer machine (see chapter 3) [155]. This was a complex procedure to produce a strong welded unit with accurately machined and faced areas to accept bearings, bushes and bolts for brake back plates, shock absorbers and driveshafts. The resulting item is almost as impressive as the aluminium components and has proved to be most resistant to normal road wear, suffering only from the usual corrosion inherent in steel underbody areas. It is not unusual for early Imps still to have their original rear suspension arms.

The completely assembled engine, transaxle and rear transmission left the unit machine workshop on an overhead conveyor to cross the central car storage area in the factory and be brought to the assembly plant [156]. It would then be installed into the Imp shell, brought from the Pressed Steel Company building on a similar conveyor, by dropping the body onto the engine assembly now on the main line. The Imp shell seen in the picture [157] has had its radiator and also its brake pipes, accelerator cable and clutch pressure pipe installed.

At the end of the assembly line the cars are driven off by competent mechanics straight into the test area for examination of all items necessary for safety and reliability—a sort of glorified MoT test. The finished car could be handed over to the customer [158], but it should be cleaned and trimmed and have its shipping protection removed from the chrome bumpers first!

157

158

12

Expansion, Exports and Later Years

IT IS said that the Imp never made money. Certainly it did not sell as well as was hoped, partly because of poor press following early teething troubles and the lack of availability of cars when the model was first released. These problems were, however, cured by 1965 with strict quality control and training of the assembly workers. Other car manufacturers had their fair share of problems, and of the competition at the time only the Ford Anglia went well right from the start. Both the Triumph Herald and the Austin Mini suffered from teething troubles. The Minis struggled and eventually succeeded through heavy marketing as a cheeky, loveable(?) second car, but the Herald would have perished had it not been for the Leyland takeover and drastic improvements to the specification.

A more severe handicap for the Imp was the lack of training of the owners, who

159

continued to ignore the servicing advice provided by the manufacturer, such as using anti-freeze or corrosion inhibitor to prevent engine deterioration. This was partly due to bad marketing, aiming for the traditional middle-of-the-road market with the small, cheap, yet very advanced product which by its nature required great care in use. Many competition successes for the Imp, however, proved that the design was good and that production was working. This was backed up by exhaustive testing (see chapter 9). It was perhaps the unusual features of the Imp which both impeded its acceptance by the conservative motoring public and also led to its being an unrivalled classic car, built far ahead of its time [159].

Acceptance of the 875cc Imp power unit, gearbox and suspension in competition and kit-car circles widened as news of the car's performance and handling spread. The engine was also carried on by Chrysler, after Imp production ended in 1976, to be used in the Sunbeam 930cc model manufactured up until 1982. Some Imps have been fitted with this slightly improved B1 engine by enthusiasts. A 930cc engine had in fact been designed by Leo Kuzmicki when a semi-automatic transmission version of the Imp was considered in 1964. The increased capacity was necessary to take up power losses in the transmission. Development capital was not sufficient to pursue this project.

Imp production, despite problems, spanned some thirteen years, and comprised a large number of models. Surely it must have had sufficient business success not to have been axed sooner, or were there other reasons? Production numbers struggled at only 10% of those of the Mini, and were so low at times that any logical planner would have closed the project down. In fact only 440,032 Imps and variants were finally produced.

Sales of Imps were not restricted to the UK, but were made throughout the world, as urged by the Government to boost exports. Even by mid-1966 the list countries to which Imps were exported consisted of Aden, Angola, Austria, Bahama, Belgium, Bermuda, Canada, Chile, Cyprus, Denmark, Dutch Guiana, Dutch West Indies, Equador, Finland, France, French West Indies, Germany, Ghana, Gibraltar, Greece, Holland, Hong Kong, Iceland, Israel, Italy, Jamaica, Japan, Kenya, Libya, Malawi, Malta, Mauritius, Mozambique, Nigeria, Norway, Okinawa, Pakistan, Panama Canal Zone, Persian Gulf, Rhodesia, Samoa, Singapore, South Vietnam, Spain, Sudan, Sweden, Switzerland, Taiwan, Tanzania, Thailand, USA, West Indies, Zambia. I have personally seen cars in several of these countries, and contacts through 'The Imp Club' extend worldwide, especially in the Netherlands and Australia, a later addition to the list.

The best-selling early model was the Imp de Luxe, originally retailed at £532. As well as selling worldwide the Imp was able to be built worldwide—from parts sent out in CKD (Completely Knocked Down) form to defray costs. Imps were built and tested at Linwood and then dismantled again for shipment. A special division of the Linwood factory was responsible for packaging up Imp 'kits' which would later be assembled in a different country. CKD Imps were exported to Austria, Costa Rica, Eire, New Zealand, the Philippines, Portugal, South Africa, Uruguay and Venezuela.

Rootes established factories in these countries to carry out the assembly work. One such in Portugal is pictured right from the earliest stages. The caption to it reads "The assembly of the spectacular Hillman Imp car will be made in Portugal, in a close Rootes-Tasso de Sousa co-operation.

"57,000 square metres of land have been acquired at Ovar, whereat a 2,100 square metre pavilion is under construction, being stage number one of this great enterprise.

"These suggestive pictures [160, 161] show a powerful caterpillar levelling 6,000 square metres of pine groves for the breakup." With completion of this factory the Imps could be produced and shipped locally as in the two pictures entitled simply 'Imps in Portugal' [162, 163].

Rootes was taken over by Chrysler in 1967, after financial difficulties, and the Imp range was remodelled. The Rootes Group was in a poor way financially from the start, and accepted a cash offer of £12.3 million in June 1964 from Chrysler, who in turn took over some 30% of Rootes Capital voting shares and 50% of ordinary non-voting shares. The Conservative Government agreed to this on the grounds that it brought dollars into the country, yet control remained with the Rootes family. As part of this preliminary agreement Rootes purchased the Pressed Steel plant at Linwood in 1966 for £14 million from BMC who had acquired it in 1965. The Chrysler takeover was fought by Tony Benn MP, Minister of Technology in the new Wilson Labour Government who instigated talks of a merger with BMC and Leyland. This was just not possible because of the level of involvement with Chrysler. The company had once again been used as a political pawn, this time in the hands of the American multinational who needed a foothold in the UK to increase its competitiveness against Ford and General Motors.

160

The new range of cars was essentially the same as the earlier ones except for differences of trim, interior and manufacturing methods which were changed to facilitate a cheaper construction. Although it was inferior to the pre-1968 models the new Imp had fared well compared to its larger relatives the Sunbeam Alpines and Tigers and the Humbers—all of which were deleted from the new range within two years. The Hunter joined the Imp on the Linwood production lines in 1969, and the Avenger was launched the following year.

Before any new products were launched there was an extensive design phase with prototypes produced and consultation between the design team, stylists and management. This culminated in an 'engineering new model brochure'. Copies of this for the Singer Chamois Coupé, Hillman Husky and Sunbeam Stiletto are available from the Imp Club. The one for the Stiletto is dated September 1967 and was the result of engineering project number 5850. The announcement date of the Stiletto was to be 2 October 1967 for export and 12 October for home consumption. It was proposed that in the year 1967/1968 2,500 of this model would be made for home sales, and 600 for export with so far no CKD cars envisaged. All the differences with other existing models were notified, together with details of body assembly, electrical system, interior, colour schemes, dimensions and performance with the complete specification and photographs of the prototype car. Acceptance of this by all parties meant that production could begin, and it would form the basis of information given to the sales department and circulated to agents.

Despite all this activity the Scottish plant never really made money for either Rootes or Chrysler. Profits and losses went up and down, but in 1974 the trend was mostly down. This is probably why the Imp line was finally dropped in 1976 in favour of cars which were cheaper to produce, such as the Sunbeam—a small-

161

sized version of the Avenger, designed to fill the gap with off-the-shelf parts. In 1977 things were no better and even a £160 million Government cash injection to prevent closure of Chrysler UK did nothing to abate the downhill trend. A last-ditch effort to keep Linwood open was made by Chrysler when they moved production of the Avenger north from Ryton in 1978. The final sale of the UK concern to the French Peugeot-Talbot Motor Company at the beginning of 1979 eventually led to the closure of Linwood in 1981.

Eighteen years from the start of 'The Dream' Linwood had become one of Scotland's most notorious industrial graveyards.

162

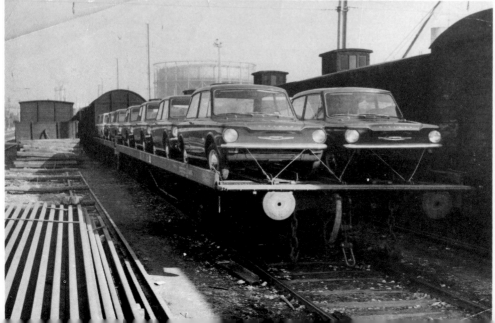

163

13

End of The Dream, and Memories

WE LEAVE Linwood by night [164, 165] with memories of the hubbub of activity inside. What has happened to this now? Was it just a dream?

There once was a factory in Scotland which, at peak rate, produced nearly 2,000 Hillman Imp motor cars a week for 13 years from 1963 until 1976. Although I never saw the factory in its prime, I have stood on the pile of rubble which was all that was left of the Pressed Steel factory in 1988 and looked across the road to the remaining frontage of the Rootes office block and showroom. The plant is now divided into several leased industrial units. I could imagine the sight of hundreds of new Imps [166–back cover] waiting to be delivered to customers via the train to Coventry and also the chatter of employees at the end of week's work.

The town of Linwood is still surrounded by the silhouette of heavy industry. There is now a rather forlorn feeling to the region where once prosperity and expansion were hoped for, but never came. Linwood did not house a new core development in regional industry as the Government had hoped, but a small producer making just one untried model existing on the periphery of the traditional network of the motor industry.

What is left behind is a memorial not to social success, but to technology, advanced production methods, and marketing. Many ideas from the Linwood project still live on and are used in modern-day cars, not only by Chrysler and Peugeot-Talbot, but by other car companies and industry who have learned their lessons from the history of industrial growth and development in the twentieth century, of which Linwood was a part. Many of the unique design features of the Imp are present in the modern hatchback Eurocars. The Imp was after all one of the first of these, with its roots deep in French, Italian and German engineering as well as British tradition, quality and inventiveness: a dream of a motor car designed by enthusiasts which serves as day-to-day transport and is equally at home on the race or rally circuit.

The question of why the Imp was never popular is the start of another story. The Henshaw brothers' book has answered it in part. The motoring public is after all unpredictable, and more influenced by bad press than good, or by hearsay more than by practical experience. In the final reckoning the Imp was just too different, and did not catch the imagination as its rivals had done, except that of the genuine car enthusiast. It was simply either loved or hated by everyone who drove it. Although the handling and performance were exceptional it was indeed

164

a specialist car requiring careful maintenance, but aimed at the low-price market. Once unfortunate rumours spread of reliability problems and production difficulties there was no hope of a comeback. This still holds true today—many innovative new products are unacceptable because their use requires a certain greater than usual attention to manufacturer's instructions.

Why was Linwood not a financial success? There is a lesson here to be learned for political planners; a hard one. Even though prosperity might have resulted from bringing unnatural employment to the Clyde Valley region it was not sufficiently backed up in terms of infrastructure. Society and industry are complex and need time to blend and grow together. This did not happen and all chances of the Imp being successful were lost. Government policy has through the nineteen-forties, 'fifties, and 'sixties dictated the development of the Linwood site for successively munitions, heavy industry and car production. The reasons for redirecting industry into areas of high unemployment are understandable, yet there remains the practical impossibility of doing this in a profitable way. Not surprisingly, production of the Hillman Imp suffered, and with change of policy the site has ceased to be of importance.

When I had my first Imp it was just one year old and still as new. This was just after production had ceased, it being a limited edition Caledonian model manufactured only between 1975-1976. Blisfully unaware of the history and prejudice attached to the car I drove it, and enjoyed driving it, uneventfully in Britain, France and Germany. I followed the standard service instructions and after eight years—three of which were on Continental roads—and around 45,000 miles, the head gasket had deteriorated. I changed it and continued driving with no further ado, and have since learned that this is quite normal for such an engine. Perhaps my success with Imps results from the fact that it was my first car, and from following the manufacturers' advice in all that I did with it, rather than using experience relevant only to other vehicles, which in any case I didn't have. The Imp is, after all, very well designed and one should expect that the manufacturers would also best understand the maintenance requirements.

I now cover around 16,000 miles per year driving Imps—an early (but rebuilt) Stiletto doing some 12,000 of that total. For newcomers to the marque there is now 'The Imp Club', a body of enthusiasts, including myself, who have built up experience of using and working on these cars and can help with questions, give hints on restoration, and supply spare parts. For further information about joining this club or on owning an Imp please contact:

> GRAHAM TOWNSEND
> *The Imp Club*
> 50 Favenfield Road
> Hambleton Park
> Thirsk
> North Yorkshire
> YO7 1FZ.

165

REFERENCES AND FURTHER READING

1   David and Peter Henshaw *Apex – The Inside Story of the Hillman Imp* 1988, 1990 (New Edition).

2   Peter Dunnett *The Decline of the British Motor Industry: the Effects of Government Policy 1945-79* 1980.

3   Rootes Group Review, special supplement *Rootes and Chrysler: a message from Lord Rootes* October 1964.

4   Stephen Young and Neil Hood *Chrysler UK: A Corporation in Transition* 1977

5   John Foster *The Clyde Valley Industrial Policy Archive: Report on Car Manufacture at Linwood* Paisley College of Technology, Politics and Sociology Department September 1983.

6   Lord Rootes' letter to Clyde Valley Industrial Policy Archive 29/10/82 (Paisley College, referenced by J. Foster)

7   Hansard Vol. 663 Cols. 709-10 *Debate on Scotland (Industry and Employment)* 19/7/62.

8   Tim Millington *Hillman Imps: tuning–overhaul–servicing* 1969, 1987, 1989

TECHNICAL NOTES
AVAILABLE FROM THE IMP CLUB

Passenger Car Technical Specification for Hillman Imp, 1963
(15 pages plus large summary sheet).

Engine Performance Curves (1956-1966).

AMA Passenger Car Specification for Hillman Imp de Luxe Mk 2, Hillman Super
Imp and Singer Chamois Mk 2, 1966 (26 pages).

AMA Passenger Car Specification for Sunbeam Sport and Stiletto, 1970
(27 pages).

Engineering New Model Brochure for Hillman Husky, 19/4/67 (16 pages).

Engineering New Model Brochure for Singer Chamois Coupé, 20/4/67 (11 pages).

Engineering New Model Brochure for Sunbeam Stiletto 2/10/67 (11 pages).

Spares List. A brochure giving up-to-date technical information and names and
addresses for further advice.

BOOKMARQUE TITLES

Hillman Imps: tuning-overhaul-servicing
Tim Millington

The Road & Christ Church Meadow
Dr Roland Newman

Apex – The Inside Story of the Hillman Imp
David & Peter Henshaw

Fiat Dino – Ferrari by another name
Mike Morris

*To Draw a Long Line – My Days with a British Sports
and Racing Car Maker: Connaught*
C E 'Johnny' Johnson

*Study & Research –
A systematic approach for students*
Dr Roland Newman

Four Brothers' '4' – The History of the Ginetta G4
Trevor Pyman

Magnificent Morris Minor
Max Horvat

*Uphill Racers –
The History of British Speed Hill Climbing*
Chris Mason

Four Wheels on my Basket (Autobiography)
Charles Meisl

Geoffrey Rootes' Dream for Linwood
Robert J Allan

Books can be ordered, in case of difficulty, direct from the Publisher at:
26 COTSWOLD CLOSE · MINSTER LOVELL · OXFORDSHIRE OX8 5SX